the new bread book

Ursula Ferrigno

photographs by Simon Wheeler

the new bread book

METRO BOOKS
NEW YORK

To Antonia, my little darling

The New Bread Book
Ursula Ferrigno

This 2008 edition published by Metro Books
by arrangement with Mitchell Beazley.

First published in Great Britain in 2007 as
The New Family Bread Book by Mitchell Beazley,
an imprint of the Octopus Publishing Group Limited
2-4 Heron Quays, London E14 4JP
An Hachette Livre UK Company

Metro Books
122 Fifth Avenue
New York, NY 10011

ISBN-13: 978-1-4351-0435-8
ISBN-10: 1-4351-0435-8

Printed and bound in China

1 3 5 7 9 10 8 6 4 2

contents

introduction

BREAD: IT'S A PLEASURE TO MAKE AND A PLEASURE TO EAT. FOR AS LONG AS I CAN REMEMBER, I HAVE FOUND MAKING AND ENJOYING BREAD ALL-ENCOMPASSING. FOR A FOOD-LOVER AND COOK, IT'S ENDLESSLY FASCINATING. THE PRIMAL INGREDIENTS CAN BE TRANSLATED INTO HUNDREDS OF DIFFERENT DELICIOUS BREADS. SOMETHING AS SIMPLE AS MORE TIME, MORE KNEADING, OR THE ADDITION OF OTHER FLOURS CAN TRANSFORM ONE TYPE OF BREAD INTO ANOTHER.

BREAD IS WHAT ONE MIGHT CALL A BASIC FOOD, AND THE SIMPLE MIXTURE OF FLOUR, WATER, SALT, AND LEAVEN (WHICH IS ALL IT IS, IN ESSENCE) IS FOUND IN EVERY SOCIETY, LARGE OR SMALL, IN THE WORLD. THOSE FEW INGREDIENTS CAN, IN COMBINATION, BE TRANSFORMED FROM VIRTUALLY NOTHING INTO SOMETHING EMINENTLY SATISFYING, WHICH SEEMS AMAZING TO ME—ALMOST LIKE MAGIC. AND WHEN BREAD-MAKING BECOMES A REGULAR ACTIVITY IN YOUR LIFE, YOU WILL PERHAPS UNDERSTAND WHY THIS FOOD IS SO INTRINSIC IN HUMAN SOCIETY. THINK OF ITS FRAGRANCE, ITS LITERAL AND METAPHORICAL WARMTH, ITS ENDLESSLY VARIED ABILITY TO PLEASE AND SUSTAIN, AND THE LOVE OF FAMILY AND FRIENDS REPRESENTED IN THE CARE AND TIME TAKEN IN ITS MAKING.

fast breads

"CARE" AND "TIME" ARE IMPORTANT WORDS IN BREAD-MAKING. MOST OF THE BREADS IN THIS BOOK ARE RELATIVELY FAST TO PREPARE AND COOK, MAKING THEM FIT EASILY INTO FAMILY LIFE. BUT BREAD-MAKING IS NEVER A TRULY FAST PROCESS; THERE ARE SIMPLY "FASTER" BREADS. IN THESE PAGES YOU'LL FIND FASTER CLASSICS FROM ITALY, FRANCE, THE UK, AND ELSEWHERE.

TYPES OF FAST BREADS

I have included lots of recipes for yeasted flatbreads and rolls, which don't take so long rising, proofing, and baking as larger loaves. But there are, of course, a few classic larger loaves, too. Many of the breads will benefit from being left to rise and proof for longer, and you can do that if you have time; I have given you ideas for how to make some of the breads more slowly. But most of the recipes here can be achieved—deliciously—in less than three hours. The non-yeast breads are particularly fast.

SLOW BREADS

The best breads you can make at home are undeniably the results of a process that is anything but conventionally fast. A true sourdough loaf could take up to four days to make, given the fermentation of the starter, the mixing, the kneading, the repeated risings, punching downs, proofing, and then baking.

Of course, one alternative to cutting down on the time spent making bread is to change your attitude to time. Bread-making may take several hours (or, occasionally, days), but it is not continuous time; it is little snippets of time, which anyone can fit into the busiest of days. The various manual stages of bread-making—the mixing, kneading, proofing, etc.—are not lengthy individually, and you can quickly learn how to make these stages fit easily into your daily life.

For instance, you can mix and knead a dough in the evening, and leave it in the refrigerator to rise overnight. If you punch it down before you go to work in the morning, you can leave it in the fridge throughout the day (and for up to two days), so long as you punch it down occasionally. In real time, you will have spent half an hour at first, plus a few minutes in each session of punching down. The dough is waiting for you to bake when you need it; it will be acquiring potential flavor and texture all the time—and I think that is what I could happily call "fast" bread. Fit bread-making into your life in a sensible way, and you'll find that it doesn't take any "time" at all.

ingredients

BREAD, IN ESSENCE, IS A SIMPLE COMBINATION OF FLOUR, LIQUID, AND A RISING AGENT SUCH AS YEAST. OTHER FLAVORINGS CAN BE ADDED, MANY OF WHICH I EXPLORE IN THE RECIPES IN THIS BOOK. I HOPE THAT BY PRACTICING THE TECHNIQUES OF BREAD-MAKING AND LEARNING HOW TO INCORPORATE DIFFERENT INGREDIENTS, YOU WILL GAIN CONFIDENCE AND START TO EXPERIMENT FOR YOURSELF.

FLOUR

Flour is the main ingredient of about three-quarters of breads. The flour you choose will give the bread its character. If it's highly refined, you will have a bland loaf, but if you use organic or stone-ground, for instance, the bread you make will be much more interesting.

WHEAT FLOURS

Most common flours are made from wheat, which consists of bran, germ, and endosperm. The bran is the husk that encloses the kernel, which is the grain: the seed in a hard shell. The nutritious wheat germ is the seed of the future plant. The endosperm, the inner part of the kernel, is full of starch and protein.

There are many varieties of wheat, the most important being *Triticum aestivum* and *Triticum durum*. Types of *Triticum aestivum* are known as "hard" or "soft" wheats. "Hardness" in wheat means that the proteins in the endosperm contain a large proportion of glutenin, the main protein that forms gluten, and, as any bread-maker knows, it is gluten that gives a bread its pleasantly elastic texture. Flours made from hard types of *Triticum aestivum* are used to make bread, while soft flours are used for pastry. *Triticum durum* is literally hard, as its Latin name suggests, and is the flour most important in the making of pasta, but it is also used in bread-making and made into semolina (and, as a grain, as couscous).

All-purpose flour (plain flour in the UK) is a blend of hard and soft wheats and can be used for breads and pastries. It has less protein and gluten than the flours specially made for bread-making.

White bread flour, called "strong white" flour in the UK, is made from hard wheat, so it has much more protein and gluten than all-purpose flour. It is very good in bread-making. Italian flours are made mostly from hard wheat and graded according to fineness: *tipo* "00" (also known as *doppio zero*) is used for fresh pasta and cakes—and occasionally breads—and *tipo* "0" is used for bread-making. In Britain, I use a very "strong" Canadian flour, made from spring wheat, which is available from good supermarkets.

Whole-wheat flour, known as "wholemeal" in the UK, is made from the complete or "whole" wheat kernel, with nothing removed. The bran and germ content make it very nutritious, but can also hinder the rising, making a much denser bread. In Britain, it can also be found in a "strong" bread-making version.

Stone-ground flour is ground slowly and gently in order to produce flour that retains all the natural goodness of the whole germ. This slow milling process only slightly warms the flour, leaving all the natural flavors and nutrients intact.

Graham flour, which is unique to the US, is made like whole-wheat (*see* page 9) but with the components (the bran, germ, and endosperm) ground separately—the endosperm is ground finely, and the other two parts ground coarsely. As a result, it is lighter and will produce a less-dense loaf than whole-wheat flour does.

Semolina flour, which is milled from the endosperm of durum wheat, comes in a couple of types: coarse semolina flour and fine semolina (or durum) flour. (The latter is also referred to in Italy as *semola di grano duro*.) Fine semolina flour is ground twice to achieve its fine texture. Both sorts are good for bread-making (though coarse semolina flour is usually best used in combination with white bread flour).

Self-rising flour is white flour with a chemical leaven such as baking powder added, which can be used in yeast-free breads. (You could make your own white self-rising at home simply by adding two level teaspoons of baking powder to each 8oz of all-purpose flour.)

Spelt flour is ground from the grains of an ancient relative of modern wheat and it has a delicious and distinctive nutty, wheaty flavor. Spelt flour contains some gluten, which makes it ideal for bread-making; the gluten, however, is more fragile and brittle than that found in conventional wheat flour, making it easier to digest.

OTHER FLOURS

A number of other grains, pulses, and vegetables are milled to produce flour. I don't use them in this book, but flours are made from millet, rice, gram (chickpeas), quinoa, buckwheat, and potato. Most of these are low in gluten, which means they produce rather dense breads, but they are ideal for those who are intolerant of wheat or gluten. However, many of them, when used in combination with wheat flours, contribute extra flavor and nutritional value.

Rye flour, ground from the whole grains of rye, is low in gluten, so breads made from rye alone are rather dense. It can be found as dark, medium, or light flour, the dark adding much more color and flavor to a bread. Mixtures of rye and wheat flours make for very tasty breads.

Corn is ground into several textures of meal: usually coarse, medium, and fine. Cornstarch is the very fine white powder used as a thickener in sauce-making (although it can be used in some cakes and cookies). Cornmeal, which is either yellow or white, can be found in a fine or coarse texture; the latter is known in Italy as *polenta* and is made into the Italian porridge also called polenta. All cornstarches are gluten-free.

Oat flour comes in various grades, distinguished by size and texture. Steel-cut or pinhead oat flour is the largest. The other most common types are medium and fine and are useful in some bread- (and cookie-) making. Oat flour does not contain gluten, but it contributes to flavor and texture when used in tandem with other bread flours.

LEAVENING AGENTS

Most of the breads in this book are leavened, or raised, by yeast, but a few use chemical leavens such as baking powder (*see* pages 146–167). There are many ways of improving the texture and flavor of the finished loaf, among them using a yeast starter, or *biga*. If you have time, I highly recommend that you try these slower methods. You will be amazed.

YEAST

This is the most commonly used leavening agent in bread-making, and it comes in several forms: fresh, active dry, and instant. Yeast is a living ingredient, whose action in bread-making is to convert the sugars in the flours into a gas (carbon dioxide), which makes the bread rise. Because it is a living organism, yeast is sensitive to heat, and the heat of the liquid used to prepare it is crucial, as is the temperature of the place where the yeasted dough is put to rise and proof (*see* pages 21 and 25). Too much heat will kill the yeast; too little will slow down its action. Yeast will survive after activation for about 20 minutes, then it needs to be mixed with flour, which provides food for its continued existence.

Fresh yeast is best because it is easier on the digestive tract and I think it produces the best flavors. It can be bought from specialist bakers' shops or from the bakery departments of some supermarkets. It should be used up fairly quickly, although it can be stored in the fridge for a couple of days. It can also be frozen for a month.

To use fresh yeast, dissolve it in whichever body-temperature liquid is called for in the recipe you are following before adding to the flour.

Active dry and **instant yeast** are fresh yeasts that have been dried and are much more concentrated than fresh, with approximately twice the potency. Active dry yeasts last much longer than fresh: for up to a year (preferably in the fridge). Instant yeast has much smaller granules than dried yeast.

To use active dry yeast, dissolve it in the body-temperature liquid called for in the recipe before adding it to the flour.

To use instant yeast, simply mix it with the flour in the bowl. When the body-temperature liquid is added, the yeast is activated.

STARTERS

"Starters" involve an alternative way of preparing the yeast when making bread. The most effective starters are sourdough, the French *levain,* and the Italian *biga.* Sourdough is perhaps the most famous, and was traditionally made by leaving a mixture of flour and water in a bowl in the kitchen or bakery for a couple of days, during which time it would ferment through the action of wild yeasts in the air. Today, most sourdough breads are made with some baker's yeast involved from the start. Breads made with these starters involve quite a lot of time and planning in advance, and you may think they have no place in a book about "fast" bread. However, you could prepare your starter a day or so before making your bread and then, really and truly, you do virtually nothing until you come to mix and knead the dough. I have given a recipe for my favorite "friend in the kitchen," the Italian *biga,* below.

Yeast starter, or *biga* As one of my students wisely said, this starter is the "turbo" in bread, an acid base that creates a greater depth of flavor and a better crust and texture. It is incorporated at the beginning stage of any bread: add 2fl oz or ¼ cup (50ml) of the starter to the well in the flour when you are adding the liquid and yeast.

To make a *biga* Sift 3½oz or ⅜ cup plus 1 tbsp (100g) strong white bread flour into a large bowl and make a well in the center. Crumble ⅙oz fresh yeast into 5fl oz or ⅝ cup (150ml) water at body temperature, then add it to the well in the flour and mix to form a batter like that needed for pancakes. It must be slack. Never rely on a recipe entirely: everything varies, depending on the flour used, the humidity, and even on the altitude (*see* pages 17 and 21), so use your judgment as well. Cover it with a damp cloth and leave it at room temperature. Keep dampening the cloth for 24 to 36 hours, but no longer. After this time, the starter will get very tangy; when you smell it, it will make your eyes water with the acidity!

A *biga* can last for at least a day in the fridge, or you can pass any leftover on to an equally enthusiastic bread-making friend. Or, as you take some *biga* out to use in a recipe, you can feed the *biga* with more flour and a small quantity of yeast. This will feed the yeast so that it is always ready for use.

Please note that you will still have to add yeast to your recipe, even if you are using a starter. And if you find there is slight separation in the starter after a day or so, don't be alarmed: simply stir it back together.

Sponge This isn't, strictly speaking, a starter, but it is a technique involving fresh or dry (but not instant) yeast, which helps the bread along much like a more conventional starter. Follow the initial steps of whichever dough recipe you are using—mixing the flour and salt, then adding the yeasted water. Draw just enough of the flour into the liquid in the well to form a soft paste, then cover it with a clean dish towel and leave it for 20-60 minutes, until the paste is frothy. Even as short a time as 20 minutes allows the yeast to ferment a little, which will improve the texture and flavor of the bread. A "fast" starter! Then incorporate the rest of the flour and continue with the recipe.

CHEMICAL LEAVENS

Chemical leavening agents were not properly discovered and perfected until the middle of the nineteenth century, but they are the primary ingredient in fast breads. Chemical leavens lose their power in storage, so they must be used fairly soon

after you buy them. Baking soda and baking powder and are the two most common agents used in domestic baking.

Baking soda is just another name for bicarbonate of soda. It is alkali, so when mixed with moisture and an acid substance, such as buttermilk or yogurt, it effervesces, producing carbon dioxide. Carbon dioxide bubbles expand with heat, and these are what cause dough to rise when baked.

Baking powder contains baking soda, but it also combines that with cream of tartar—a built-in acidifying agent—and a drying agent: usually cornstarch. It comes as single-acting or double-acting. Single-acting powders react instantly to moisture, so breads made with them must be baked immediately after mixing. Double-acting powders react in two phases, so any recipe containing them can stand for a while before baking.

LIQUIDS

Liquid is vital in bread-making. If it is at the right temperature, it activates the yeast and starts the whole process of leavening. Without liquid, the flour could not be made into a dough. Water is the most common liquid and I prefer to use spring or bottled still waters; these contain fewer additives and are generally lighter and more pure than tap water (London water may be fine to drink, for instance, but it has a flavor and this will affect bread). Other bread-making liquids include milk, buttermilk, yogurt, even beer and wine occasionally, and all give a dough its unique consistency, texture, and flavor.

Water should be added to yeast at around body temperature: 98.6°F. You can use a thermometer for this, but an easier way is to mix two-thirds cold water with one-third boiling water.

SALT

Salt is primarily used in breads to add flavor but it also has another important role to play. It inhibits yeast fermentation, which strengthens the developing gluten, making for a better bread that lasts longer. Use natural sea salt for the best flavor (which won't complicate the bread with the extra additives that a free-running salt contains). I use a fine sea salt, but if you can find only coarse (which is useful for a bread topping occasionally), crush it using a mortar and pestle.

SUGAR

Sugar used to be important in bread-making because it was used as a "food" for the yeast, but modern yeasts do not require sugar to become active. Sugar (usually granulated) is still used, though, even in savory breads, because it enhances flavor, texture, and the color of the crust. Honey, maple syrup, and molasses can substitute for sugar in some breads.

ENRICHING INGREDIENTS

Fats such as butter, oils, milk, and eggs are the primary bread-enriching ingredients. Fat coats the gluten strands in the dough, which slows down yeast fermentation, making for a better bread with a better flavor that lasts longer. Enriched breads are usually softer in crumb and can even be quite cake-like, depending on the amount of butter and eggs used.

Use the best-possible enriching ingredients: good olive oil, preferably extra-virgin; a single vegetable oil such as sunflower or safflower; unsalted butter; and fresh, large, preferably organic eggs.

bread-making techniques

MEASURING, MIXING AND KNEADING ARE QUITE DIFFERENT TECHNIQUES. ACCURATE MEASURING IS CRUCIAL, AND CAN BE TRICKIER THAN IT SEEMS. MIXING IS THE NEXT STAGE, WHEN YOU ARE BLENDING THE BASIC INGREDIENTS TOGETHER INTO A DOUGH; ONLY THEN DO YOU KNEAD IT. KNEADING IS REALLY GOOD, BLOOD-PUMPING, CARDIO-VASCULAR EXERCISE THAT DISTRIBUTES THE YEAST AND DEVELOPS THE GLUTEN. IT HELPS GET RID OF THOSE "CHICKEN WINGS" UNDER YOUR ARMS, TOO, SO IT IS GOOD FOR YOU AS WELL AS YOUR BREAD.

MEASURING

Measuring flour is all-important in bread-making. The US cup system of measurement is convenient, but it is nearly impossible to achieve the consistent measures of flour with it that will guarantee a perfect result each time. As any bread-baker will tell you, even the same cook using the same cup measure gets a different weight of flour each time that cup is filled, due to the fickle nature of flour: it absorbs moisture from the air, so is easily affected by weather and altitude; different types and brands have different specific gravities; its weight will vary greatly depending on whether you spoon it or scoop it into the cup.

I always use a set of metric scales to weigh out ingredients carefully, because the correct proportions are crucial—and all the recipes in this book take their original measurements from those scales. While both ounce and cup measures have also been included here, do note that the cup measures are only approximate—there is no absolutely standard conversion from metric to ounces, let alone from metric to cup measures. If you already own a set of kitchen scales, I advise you to use those and follow the ounce measurements, or else invest in a good set; these days, digital ones using both metric and ounces are easily available (and affordable) by mail-order or online.

MIXING

For mixing, you need a large bowl (preferably glass, so that you can see what is happening more easily) and a good wooden spoon. Combine the flour and salt in the bowl and make a well in the center with the wooden spoon. Pour the yeasted water (usually only a proportion of the water specified) and any starter into the well. Start to draw the flour in from the sides of the bowl, mixing with the liquid, until you have a stiff paste. Before mixing in all the flour, you can leave a paste in the well to "sponge" (*see* page 13).

Bit by bit, gradually pour in a proportion of the remaining water, still mixing in the remaining flour from around the well. The texture of the paste will loosen, but be careful with the water additions—you don't want the dough to be too wet, and so much can affect the ability of the flour to absorb liquid. Some flours will absorb liquid more readily than others, and on a humid day a flour will absorb less liquid than it will on a dry day. Never add all the liquid at once.

Mix, adding water only until the consistency of the dough is as specified in the recipe: usually firm, soft, or "raggy" (rough-textured)—not sticky, but not too dry. Damp is probably best.

KNEADING

Kneading enables the yeast to be distributed evenly throughout the dough and also helps the proteins in the flour to develop into gluten. The starches in the flour are broken down; these feed the yeast, and then the bubbles of carbon dioxide created by the yeast help the dough to rise. As a general rule of thumb, the more you knead, the less flavor a bread will have. Ironically, however, every bread needs to be kneaded.

Bought bread (or bread made in an electric machine) is never kneaded; it's just mixed. That is why it is less digestible: the proteins are not distributed well enough in the dough. There will be none of that familiar "bloating" if you eat homemade bread that has been kneaded well before baking.

Your work surface needs to be lightly floured—what the industry calls "bench flour." You could keep a little pile of flour to the side, just in case you need more.

FIRM DOUGHS

Put a firm dough on the surface and fold it in half towards you. Using the heel of your hand, push the dough away from you, at the same time using your other hand to rotate it slightly towards you. Continue this folding, pushing, and rotating (and adding a little more flour if the dough is sticky) for the kneading time specified in the recipe—usually about ten minutes. The dough will change texture, becoming firm, smooth, silky to the touch, and elastic. You could try the stretch test to see if the dough is ready (*see* right), then shape it into a ball for rising (*see* page 21).

SOFT, RAGGY DOUGHS

Doughs that are softer and damper need a slightly different treatment. Flour the board as above, perhaps a little more generously, and use a plastic dough scraper to turn the dough (your hands would get impossibly sticky). The dough will remain soft and pliable after kneading but will have lost its stickiness. This "kneading" allows the bread to be lighter when it is baked, which means it is lighter on the digestion.

KNEADING IN OTHER INGREDIENTS

Many of the breads in this book contain coarser ingredients that need to be added later than the mixing stage. These include chopped nuts, vegetable purées, seeds, and dried fruit. Knead the bread for a few minutes, then leave it to rest for another few minutes. Press the dough into a round and top it with the ingredient(s) to be included. Fold the dough in half, then gently knead it until the added ingredient is evenly distributed. The dough will look a bit crumbly at one point but it will come together smoothly after about three minutes' kneading. Or you could "chafe in" the ingredients (*see* page 22) just before proofing, which I think gives a lighter texture than kneading.

STRETCH TEST

To check whether a dough has been kneaded enough for the gluten to develop elasticity, stretch a large-ish piece of it between your fingers. It should behave like a piece of blown bubblegum and be thin, even, translucent, and not ripping or breaking. This is what I call the stretch test, and it is vital when making breads. Some people call it the "windowpane test," meaning that you can stretch the dough enough without breaking to enable you to see through it.

RISING

The speed of rising will depend on temperature and humidity as well as on factors such as type of flour and starter (if any). Dough will rise faster on a warm, humid day than on a cool, dry one, for instance. A warm to cool kitchen, away from draughts, is the best. But on a very hot day, you might need to put a rising dough in a cooler environment—a cold pantry or the bathroom, for instance, or even the garage or basement. On a very cold day, you could put the bowl of dough near a central-heating vent, near the hot-water heater, or even in the oven with the oven light on.

Altitude can make a difference, too. Really fast bread could be made at high altitudes: above 3,500ft, a low atmospheric pressure causes bread dough to rise and proof more quickly than is indicated in many conventional recipes. Even if you live in a fourth-floor apartment, you might have to revise the timings of a recipe for much the same reason.

Put the dough in a glass bowl that is large enough to allow the dough to double in size (metal is not suitable because it might conduct too much heat). Cover the dough and leave it to rise for the time recommended in the recipe you are following. A clean, damp dish towel is usually ideal, but now and again you might need something warmer, such as plastic wrap. Because plastic wrap is so impermeable, if you stretch it across the top of the bowl it will speed things up, encouraging the yeast to reproduce more speedily. But be careful: plastic wrap creates such a warm environment, trapping everything inside, that dough can overdevelop.

When the dough is ready, it will have visibly doubled in size and there will be air bubbles on its surface. To check that rising is complete, press a finger into the middle of the dough: the indentation will spring back slowly if the dough is ready, immediately if the dough is under-risen, and it won't spring back at all if it is over-risen.

You can put a dough to rise in the fridge, where it will adapt to the cooler temperature, giving a very slow but very even rise and encouraging flavor. This is a prime example of how you can make bread-making fit into your own life, saving precious time. But you must bring the dough back to room temperature before baking it, during which time it will puff up even more. A cold dough put straight into the oven would produce a heavy, dense bread.

PUNCHING DOWN

"Punching down" means deflating the dough to get rid of trapped gas. If this gas produced by the yeast were to carry on growing, the dough would eventually collapse. Punching down enables the process to begin again, all the time improving flavor and strengthening crust and crumb.

Press down into the dough with your knuckles and it will visibly diminish in size. Turn it out onto a lightly floured work surface and knead it as recommended in the recipe you are following, then leave the dough to rest and relax for a few minutes before shaping and/or proofing it.

One of my best *focaccias* came about when I had no time at all. I had made the dough, but just couldn't find a minute to bake it, so I kept on punching it down, letting it rise, then punching it down again. I think I went on like this for a couple of days and the flavor and texture, once the dough was baked, were incredible. If you are not ready to bake, the dough will wait, so long as you keep punching it down. Let it fit into your life—not the other way around.

CHAFING

To chafe, apply a light, downward pressure to the sides of the round ball of dough while simultaneously rotating the dough continuously in a steady, clockwise motion. This lightens the bread, expanding and lengthening the bubbles of air in it—it's particularly effective with *focaccia*. After a good chafe, a cross-section of baked bread will have a honeycomb-like texture. Chafing should also be used when you need to incorporate added ingredients into a dough (walnuts, for instance; *see* page 18). It will encourage your bread to be lighter and will also help distribute the ingredients more evenly. Put the ingredients on top of your ball of dough, press them in slightly, then chafe them in.

SHAPING AND PROOFING

When the dough has been punched down and rested, it is ready to be shaped and proofed.

SHAPING LOAVES

Round loaf Cup your hands around the risen and punched-down ball of dough and press your fingers into its base. Rotate the dough, applying pressure with your cupped hands to shape it into a round. Continue until you have a smooth, round shape. If you turn the dough over, there should be an indentation in the center when it is ready. Place it on a baking sheet.

Oval loaf First, create a round as above, then cup your hands around the loaf and apply pressure until you have a torpedo shape.

Long loaf Press the risen and punched-down ball of dough into a flat round. Fold one edge of the dough into the center. Fold the other half on top. Seal the folds on the three edges of the loaf. In the center of the long side of the dough, press to make an indentation all the way along. Roll it under your palms until you have the desired length.

Couronne (**crown loaf**) Shape the risen and punched-down dough into a round, then flatten it. Use the heel of your hand to press an indentation into the center of the dough, right down to the work surface. Push your hands into the indentation and through to the work surface, and slowly push the dough out, using the backs of your hands to create a ring shape about eight inches across.

SHAPING ROLLS

Round rolls Divide the risen dough into small pieces, just large enough to fit in the palm of your hand. Roll each piece of dough on a floured surface, pressing out the air, until you have a round.

PROOFING

This is the final rise, in a prepared loaf pan or on a prepared baking sheet, which is done after the dough has been shaped (and during which time you can preheat the oven). The temperature should be similar to that of the first rising: warm to cool and draught-free. Leave the dough for the recommended time but no longer, because you do not want it to over-proof, which can be disastrous. When the dough is ready, it will have visibly increased in size and will feel spongy rather than firm. A finger indentation will spring back slowly. The dough is now ready to be glazed or topped (if not already done) and then baked.

GLAZING AND TOPPING

Bread and rolls are usually glazed after proofing, but sometimes it is done before; follow the instructions in the recipe you are using. Occasionally, glazes are applied before and after baking, and some toppings are added halfway through baking. The glaze is often needed as a glue for the topping. It all depends on the effect desired.

GLAZES

Glazing before baking adds color, flavor, and potential texture to the crust; glazing after baking adds color and flavor and usually softens the texture of the crust.

If you are glazing the loaf before baking it, put your chosen glaze in a small bowl and paint it onto the top surfaces of the unbaked, proofed bread or rolls using a soft pastry brush. If you are glazing after baking, apply the glaze in the same way while the bread is still warm.

Possible glazes include: water, milk, egg; milk and egg; egg yolk and salt; milk and sugar; honey; maple syrup; salted water; and olive oil.

TOPPINGS

Toppings are a delicious extra for breads and rolls, sometimes echoing the ingredient that has been kneaded in and sometimes introducing a new texture and flavor. Toppings can also make bread and rolls look more interesting. Remember that, to adhere, most toppings should be put onto a glaze.

Possible toppings include: extra flour, coarse sea salt, whole or ground spices (paprika, cumin, poppy seeds, and sunflower seeds), fresh herbs, grains (cracked wheat, bran flakes, rolled oats, and cornmeal), grated cheese, chopped nuts, sugars, and chopped dried fruit for sweet breads.

BAKING

You should "know" your oven: where it is hottest and where it is coolest. This will help you work out whether the shelf should be higher or lower, or whether the bread needs to be turned around halfway through cooking.

PREPARING THE OVEN

First, preheat the oven to the right temperature. This probably needs 20 minutes or so and can be done while the bread is proofing.

Steam There are some techniques that can help particular breads. Steam plays an important role in baking many breads; it helps soften the crust initially, helping it to rise more, and also helps it to become golden brown. There are a couple of ways in which steam can be created. You could spray the sides of the preheated oven with a water sprayer as you put the bread into it (and do so a couple of times during the baking). Or you could put a roasting pan with a film of water or a couple of ice cubes in it on the base

of the oven. Don't add any more water—this will steam the bread too much and make the crust far too soft (sometimes virtually no crust). Put the roasting pan into the oven a few minutes before you add the bread.

Preheating baking sheets/tiles/pizza stones Many breads respond best when baked directly on a heat source, such as a preheated baking sheet or a preheated unglazed ceramic tile. The pizza is a case in point: the base becomes very much more crisp when cooked on a preheated pizza stone.

PREPARING THE PROOFED DOUGH

Slashing, cutting, or prodding a dough is done for decorative and functional reasons. If you cut or slash, you allow the bread to rise and expand without tearing elsewhere—and you also get more crust, which I think is always to be desired!

A scalpel (you can get them from kitchen or art suppliers) is a good, clean blade to use. Otherwise, use a pair of sharp scissors.

PUTTING DOUGH INTO THE OVEN

Put your baking sheet or loaf pan into the preheated oven and close the door quickly. In the first few minutes of baking, the oven's heat turns the moisture in the dough into steam, causing the loaf to rise rapidly. The heat then deactivates the yeast, which allows the crust to solidify and become golden.

Follow the recommended baking times carefully (depending on your oven, of course) and keep an eye on the bread: if it is browning too much on one side, turn it around. Try not to open the door too much, however. That said, when you are baking rolls, opening the oven door slightly for the last five minutes sometimes makes the rolls crisper.

TAKING BREAD OUT OF THE OVEN

The first thing to do is test that the bread is done—if, of course, it is not in a loaf pan. Tap the base with your fingertips; it should make a hollow sound.

Place the bread or rolls on a wire rack. If the loaf is in a pan, turn it out onto the rack to cool; the crumb will collapse if it's left inside the pan with steam and become gooey, almost like raw dough.

And do try to leave the bread to cool. I know it's tempting, but I don't think it's very good for us to eat bread that is too warm. Bread is also easier to cut when it is cooler.

STORING AND FREEZING

Make double quantities of any dough and freeze half of it for up to six months. Most breads are eaten immediately, but you can freeze them (whole or in portions): wrap them in foil or special freezer bags (get rid of air first) and seal them well. You can then defrost the bread naturally or in the microwave—and there you have "fast" bread.

To keep bread at home, wrap it in brown paper and store it in a bread box or crock. You can also keep it in the fridge, but I don't particularly like cold bread.

You can also freeze fresh yeast, but make sure you defrost it thoroughly before use (it will become liquid). Use double quantities in exactly the same way as you would with unfrozen fresh yeast.

BREAD-MAKING MACHINES

A bread machine can mix, rise, and bake a loaf. Many manufacturers will tell you that it kneads the bread, too, but no machine can stretch the dough as the human hand can. However good the paddles of a mixer, all they do to a dough is mix it rather than knead it, and kneading is vitally important—as you will find out. Consequently, machine-made bread tends to be more dense because the gluten hasn't been fully stretched. If your hands are in good repair, you don't need to use a machine—and think what a good workout you will have from all that kneading! A second problem is that an electric bread-maker steams a bread rather than baking it. Most of the recipes in this book can be made using a bread machine, but you need to use either a yeast made especially for bread machines or an instant yeast.

There are many types of bread machines, and the order in which you add the ingredients to the machine depends on the type you have. Add the ingredients to the baking cylinder and then put it inside the machine, choose a setting, and flick the start switch. After the machine has been mixing for ten minutes, check the dough. Add a little water if it is too soft; add a little flour if it is too stiff. Add any extra ingredients, such as peel or nuts, shortly before the end of the mixing stage.

Close the lid when the rising begins and leave it closed until the loaf is baked. Then turn the loaf out of the pan and leave it to cool on a wire rack.

classic breads

THE BREADS IN THIS CHAPTER ARE THOSE THAT ARE MOST EASILY RECOGNIZED; ON THE WHOLE, THEY ARE SIMPLE, STRAIGHTFORWARD RECIPES. THESE BREADS CAN ACCOMPANY AN ARRAY OF DAILY DISHES AND SERVE A MULTITUDE OF PURPOSES. SOME OF THEM MAY TAKE TIME TO MAKE, BUT (AND THIS IS A RECURRING THEME OF THIS BOOK) THE INDIVIDUAL STAGES OF BREAD-MAKING—THE MIXING, KNEADING, PROOFING, AND SO ON—ARE NOT LENGTHY, AND YOU WILL QUICKLY LEARN HOW TO MAKE THESE STAGES FIT EASILY INTO YOUR DAILY LIFE.

THESE ARE THE BREADS THAT I THINK YOU WILL RETURN TO MOST OFTEN. ONCE YOU HAVE MASTERED THEM
AND GAINED CONFIDENCE (A VITAL ELEMENT OF BREAD-MAKING), YOU MAY BECOME INCLINED TO EXPERIMENT AND
TRY ADAPTING THE RECIPES WITH YOUR OWN IDEAS—ANOTHER HUGELY IMPORTANT FACTOR IN BREAD-MAKING.

THERE ARE MANY DIFFERENT TYPES OF BREAD HERE, FROM BRITAIN, FRANCE, AND, OF COURSE, ITALY, TOGETHER
WITH SOME FROM THE USA AND THE MIDDLE EAST. I HOPE YOU ENJOY THEM ALL.

pain de campagne

BLENDING DIFFERENT FLOURS CAN CREATE GREAT TEXTURES AND FLAVORS, AND THIS BREAD IS A CLASSIC EXAMPLE. THE RYE FLOUR, FOR INSTANCE, STARTS TO FERMENT SLIGHTLY AS IT RISES, ADDING FLAVOR AND A GOOD CRUST. MOST FRENCH COUNTRY LOAVES ARE MADE WITH A STARTER (*SEE* VARIATION BELOW), BUT THIS WORKS WELL WITHOUT.

14OZ OR 2⅗ CUPS (400G) WHITE BREAD FLOUR

4OZ OR 1 CUP + 1 TBSP (115G) RYE FLOUR

1 TBSP FINE SEA SALT

2OZ OR 4 TBSP (55G) UNSALTED BUTTER, SOFTENED
   AND DICED

1OZ (25G) FRESH YEAST, CRUMBLED

10FL OZ OR 1¼ CUPS (300ML) WATER AT
   BODY TEMPERATURE

1 Put the flours and salt into a large bowl and rub in the butter until the mixture resembles fine bread crumbs. Cream the yeast with 2 tbsp of the water in a small bowl. Make a well in the center of the flour and add the yeast and enough of the remaining water to make a soft dough.

2 Tip the dough out onto a lightly floured surface and knead for 5 minutes, until it is smooth and elastic. Place it in a lightly oiled bowl, cover with a damp dish towel, and leave to rise for 1 hour, until doubled in size.

3 Punch down the dough, tip it out onto a lightly floured surface, and knead for 2-3 minutes. Shape it into a ball, then slightly flatten the top and dust with flour. Using a sharp knife, mark out a square on top of the dough. Place it on a greased baking sheet, cover it with a damp dish towel, and leave to proof for 1 hour, or until it has doubled in size. Preheat the oven to 425°F.

4 Bake the loaf for 25–30 minutes until it is golden brown and the base of the loaf sounds hollow when tapped with the fingertips. Cool on a wire rack.

slow variation

You could make this loaf with a starter for enhanced flavor. Add a half-recipe *biga* (*see* page 12) to the well in the flour with the recipe yeast and water, then continue as described above.

classic white loaf

THIS IS A CLASSIC BRITISH WHITE LOAF, MADE WITH MILK FOR A SOFTER CRUMB. IF YOU LIKE, YOU CAN MAKE ABOUT SEVEN CUTS IN THE TOP AND BRUSH IT ALL OVER WITH AN EGG-AND-WATER GLAZE. THEN YOU CAN SPRINKLE IT WITH A COMBINATION OF SESAME, PUMPKIN, AND SUNFLOWER SEEDS.

1LB OR 3⅕ CUPS (450G) WHITE BREAD FLOUR

2 TSP FINE SEA SALT

1 TBSP SUPERFINE SUGAR

2OZ OR 4 TBSP (55G) UNSALTED BUTTER, SOFTENED AND DICED

½OZ (15G) FRESH YEAST, CRUMBLED

10FL OZ OR 1¼ CUPS (300ML) WHOLE MILK AT BODY TEMPERATURE

1 Sift the flour and salt into a large bowl and stir in the sugar. Rub in the butter until the texture is like bread crumbs, then make a well in the center. Cream the yeast with 2 tbsp of the milk, then pour it into the well in the flour, along with enough of the remaining milk to mix to a smooth and elastic dough.

2 Knead the dough on a lightly floured surface for 5 minutes, until it is smooth. Leave it to rise in a lightly oiled bowl, covered with a damp dish towel, for 1 hour or until it has doubled in size.

3 Preheat the oven to 400°F and lightly oil a 2lb loaf pan.

4 Punch down the dough, then turn it onto a lightly floured surface and knead it for 5 more minutes. Roll the dough into a round, cupping your hands around the sides, and ease it into the prepared loaf pan. Cover with the dish towel and leave to proof for 10 minutes.

5 Dust with extra flour and bake for 30-35 minutes, until the loaf is golden. Turn it out of the pan and cool it on a wire rack.

variation
You can make the dough into dinner rolls. After punching down, divide the dough into 12 equal pieces and shape it into balls. Space them well apart on an oiled baking sheet, and bake for 20-25 minutes.

whole-wheat bread

THIS BREAD IS EASY, QUICK AND DELICIOUS. EAT IT WITH SOUP OR TOASTED FOR BREAKFAST, OR USE IT TO MAKE SANDWICHES. YOU CAN ALSO USE IT TO MAKE CRUMBS FOR USE IN THE BROWN-BREAD ICE CREAM RECIPE ON PAGE 187.

1 Put the flours and salt into a large bowl and make a well in the center. Cream the yeast with 1 tbsp of the milk and water. Pour into the well in the flour and mix until the dough comes away from the sides of the bowl.

2 Tip the dough out onto a lightly floured surface and knead for 5 minutes, until it is smooth and elastic. Place the dough in a lightly oiled bowl, cover with a damp dish towel, and leave to rise for 45 minutes in a warm place, until it is doubled in size.

3 Preheat the oven to 425°F.

4 Knock down, then turn the dough out onto a floured surface and knead once more for 5 minutes. Shape the dough into a round and place on a greased baking sheet. Brush the surface of the loaf with water and sprinkle with the rolled oats. Cover with a dish towel, and leave to proof for 15-20 minutes.

5 Bake the bread for 15–20 minutes, until it is golden and the base of the bread sounds hollow when tapped with the fingertips. Cool on a wire rack.

variation

You can make whole-wheat rolls from this dough. Divide the dough into 12 pieces and form into rounds (or whatever shape you like). Bake for 10–12 minutes.

DOUGH

8OZ OR 2 CUPS (220G) GRAHAM FLOUR

4OZ OR 1 CUP (120G) WHOLE-WHEAT FLOUR

4OZ OR ⅘ CUP (115G) WHITE BREAD FLOUR

2 TSP FINE SEA SALT

½OZ (15G) FRESH YEAST, CRUMBLED

10FL OZ OR 1¼ CUPS (300ML) MILK AND WATER,
    AT BODY TEMPERATURE, MIXED

TOPPING

1 TBSP WATER

1 TBSP WHOLE ROLLED OATS

classical focaccia

FOCACCIA GETS ITS NAME FROM THE LATIN WORD FOR "HEARTH", *FOCUS*. THIS RECIPE TOOK THE LONGEST TO RESEARCH. THE *FOCACCIA* I MADE AS A TEENAGER WAS MUCH SIMPLER, BUT THIS ONE HAS IMPROVED ENORMOUSLY. THIS IS DUE PARTLY TO EXPERIENCE AND PRACTICE, AND PARTLY TO UNDERSTANDING THE CHEMICAL PROCESSES INVOLVED. ALTHOUGH IT'S SLIGHTLY MORE COMPLICATED AND LENGTHY THAN THE *FOCACCIA* ON PAGE 36, I HOPE YOU LIKE IT.

1 Mix the flour and salt in a large bowl and run your hands through the flour to warm it a little. Make a well in the center. Dissolve the yeast in 2 tbsp of the water and add this to the well, along with 1 tbsp of the oil and the *biga*. With a wooden spoon, add the remaining water little by little until you get a raggy dough that is not too wet and not too dry.

2 Turn the dough out onto a lightly floured work surface and knead well for 10 minutes. Use the stretch test (*see* page 18) to check that it is ready. Return the kneaded dough to a clean, oiled bowl and rub a little oil on top of it. Cover with a damp dish towel and leave to rise for 1¼ hours.

3 Uncover the dough, punch it down, and knead for 5 minutes. Cover again with the damp cloth and leave to rest for 10 minutes.

4 Roll the dough out into a round or square at least a half-inch thick. Place it on an oiled baking sheet, cover with the damp dish towel, and leave to proof for 30 minutes.

5 Preheat the oven to 400°F.

6 Using your fingertips, dimple the dough, then sprinkle it with coarse salt and pepper and the rosemary. Leave to rest for 10 minutes.

7 Bake the dough in the middle of the oven for 30 minutes, until golden brown. Remove from the oven and place on a wire rack to cool. When it is cool, anoint it with the finest extra-virgin olive oil, cut it into wedges, and enjoy.

DOUGH

9OZ OR 1⅘ CUPS (250G) WHITE BREAD FLOUR

2 TSP FINE SEA SALT

¼OZ (10G) FRESH YEAST, CRUMBLED

APPROX. 7FL OZ OR ⅞ CUP (200ML) WATER AT
    BODY TEMPERATURE

OLIVE OIL

3 TBSP *BIGA* (*SEE* PAGE 12)

FINISH

COARSE SEA SALT

COARSELY GROUND BLACK PEPPER

LEAVES FROM 2-3 SPRIGS FRESH ROSEMARY

EXTRA-VIRGIN OLIVE OIL

simple focaccia

THIS SIMPLER VERSION OF THE CLASSIC BREAD ON PAGE 35 IS FOUND THROUGHOUT ITALY AND VARIES FROM REGION TO REGION BY THE ADDITION OF A SIMPLE SEASONED TOPPING OR A FILLING. THIS ONE IS TOPPED WITH CRUSHED GARLIC AND ROSEMARY AND IS MY FAVORITE. IT IS TRADITIONALLY EATEN AS A SNACK.

DOUGH

8OZ OR 1⅘ CUPS (225G) WHITE BREAD FLOUR

1 TSP FINE SEA SALT

½OZ (15G) FRESH YEAST, CRUMBLED

6½FL OZ OR ¾ CUP + 1 TBSP (185ML) WATER AT BODY TEMPERATURE

OLIVE OIL

FINISH

1 GARLIC CLOVE

COARSE SEA SALT

2 TSP DRIED ROSEMARY

1 Put the flour on a clean work surface. Gently mix in the salt, then form into a mound with a well in the center. Cream the yeast with 3 tbsp of the water. Pour the yeast liquid into the hollow in the flour and carefully fold the flour over it, then add 3 tbsp of the olive oil. Add enough of the remaining water to make a stiff but pliable dough.

2 Knead the dough on a lightly floured surface for 10–15 minutes. Put it in a lightly oiled bowl and cover with a damp dish towel. Leave it in a warm place for about 30 minutes, until it has doubled in size.

3 Preheat the oven to 425°F. Brush a baking sheet with some of the olive oil. Peel and crush the garlic and steep it in about 1 tbsp of olive oil.

4 Punch down the dough, then knead it for 2–3 minutes on a lightly floured surface. Roll out to a round about a quarter-inch thick. Place the dough on the oiled baking sheet. Brush the garlic and oil onto the dough and sprinkle with coarse sea salt and dried rosemary. Cover and leave to proof for 10 minutes.

5 Bake for 10 minutes, then reduce the heat to 375°F and bake for a further 20 minutes. Serve hot.

couronne

THIS BREAD—ITS FRENCH NAME MEANS "CROWN"—WAS SHAPED IN A CIRCLE SO THAT HOUSEWIVES COULD CARRY IT EASILY ON THEIR ARMS FROM THE MARKET. THE RECIPE BELOW IS A CHEAT'S VERSION, WHICH WOULD TRADITIONALLY BE MADE USING A STARTER DOUGH SUCH AS THE *BIGA* ON PAGE 12 (*SEE* VARIATION BELOW).

1 Sift the flour and salt into a large bowl and make a well in the center. In a separate small bowl, cream the yeast and sugar with 1 tbsp of the water. Add the yeast mixture and yogurt to the well in the flour, with enough of the water to make a soft dough.

2 Tip the dough out onto a lightly floured surface and knead for 5 minutes, until it is smooth and elastic. Place it in a lightly oiled bowl, cover with a damp dish towel, and leave it to rise for 45 minutes, or until it has doubled in size.

3 Punch down the dough, then tip it onto a lightly floured surface and knead for 2-3 minutes. Shape it into an 8-inch round and make a hole in the center about 5 inches wide. Place the dough on a lightly greased baking sheet and make 3 or 4 diagonal cuts around the edge

of the ring, which will open out like a crown. Grease the outside of a small bowl and place it in the center of the bread to keep the shape. Leave it to proof, covered with a damp dish towel, for 30 minutes, or until it has doubled in size.

4 Preheat the oven to 425°F.

5 Remove the bowl and dust the loaf lightly with extra flour. Bake for 20-25 minutes, until it is well risen and golden and the base of the bread sounds hollow when tapped with the fingertips. Cool on a wire rack.

slow variation

A starter will enhance the flavor of the bread. Add a half-recipe *biga* to the well in the flour along with the yeast, yogurt, and water. Continue as described above.

18OZ OR 3⅗ CUPS (500G) WHITE BREAD FLOUR

1½ TSP FINE SEA SALT

¾OZ (20G) FRESH YEAST, CRUMBLED

2 TSP SUPERFINE SUGAR

6FL OZ OR ¾ CUP (175ML) WATER AT
    BODY TEMPERATURE

7OZ OR ⅞ CUP(200G) NATURAL YOGURT

pain d'epi

THIS FRENCH BREAD WOULD BE MADE TRADITIONALLY USING A STARTER DOUGH MADE THE DAY BEFORE (*SEE* VARIATION BELOW), BUT I HAVE SHORTENED THE PROCESS. THE BREAD IS CUT SEVERAL TIMES SO THAT THE FINISHED LOAF RESEMBLES A SPIKE OF WHEAT. THE DOUGH CAN ALSO BE USED TO MAKE SIMPLE BAGUETTES.

18OZ OR 3⅗ CUPS (500G) WHITE BREAD FLOUR

1 TBSP FINE SEA SALT

¾OZ (20G) FRESH YEAST, CRUMBLED

10FL OZ OR 1¼ CUPS (300ML) WATER AT
    BODY TEMPERATURE

1 Put the flour and salt into a large bowl and make a well in the center. Cream the yeast with 1 tbsp of the water and add it, bit by bit, to the well in the flour with the remaining water. Mix until the dough comes away from the sides of the bowl.

2 Tip the dough onto a lightly floured surface and knead it for 5 minutes, until it is smooth. Place the dough in a lightly oiled bowl, cover with a damp dish towel, and leave to rise for 1 hour, until it has doubled in size.

3 Punch down the dough, then tip it out onto a lightly floured surface and knead it for 2-3 minutes. Shape it into a baguette and place it on a lightly greased baking sheet. Using sharp scissors, make diagonal cuts halfway through the dough down each side, placing the cut flaps on alternate sides so that the loaf resembles a spike of wheat. Cover with a damp dish towel and leave to proof for 1 hour.

4 Preheat the oven to 425°F.

5 Bake the loaf for 25–30 minutes, until it is golden and the base of the bread sounds hollow when tapped with your fingertips. Leave it to cool on a wire rack.

slow variation

You can of course use a starter. Use a half-recipe of *biga* (*see* page 12), adding it to the well in the flour with the yeast and water. Continue as described above.

music-sheet bread

THIS SPECIAL SARDINIAN BREAD IS KNOWN AS *CARTA DA MUSICA,* OR "MUSIC-SHEET BREAD," BECAUSE IT SHOULD BE THIN ENOUGH FOR YOU TO READ MUSIC THROUGH IT. IT WAS ONCE A FOOD FOR THE SHEPHERDS: THEY MIGHT SOFTEN IT IN EWES MILK, CRUMBLE IT UP, AND DRIZZLE IT WITH HONEY FOR BREAKFAST, OR SOFTEN IT IN WATER AND FILL IT WITH VEGETABLES BEFORE BAKING IT OVER THE FIRE AS A PANCAKE FOR LUNCH.

2¼LB OR APPROXIMATELY 9 CUPS (1KG) FINE SEMOLINA FLOUR

¼OZ (10G) FRESH YEAST, CRUMBLED

1 TSP COARSE SEA SALT

ABOUT 12FL OZ OR 1½ CUPS (350ML) WATER AT BODY TEMPERATURE

1 Put the flour on a work surface and make a well in the middle. Dissolve the yeast and the salt separately, each in 2 tbsp of the water. Add the yeast liquid to the well with the salty water and the remaining water, and mix to a dough.

2 Knead the dough on a lightly floured surface for about 10 minutes, until it is soft, damp, and smooth. Shape it into eight balls about 3¼ inches in diameter, cover with a damp dish towel, and leave to rise for about 2 hours in a dry place.

3 Preheat the oven to 400°F.

4 Punch down the dough and knead it for 2–3 minutes on a lightly floured surface. Roll out the individual pieces of dough, keeping them constantly floured so they do not stick, to obtain circles of about ¹⁄₁₆–⅛-inch thickness and 16 inches in diameter.

5 Cook the sheets of dough, one on top of the other—all eight at the same time—in the preheated oven, and separate them only when they begin to swell.

6 At this point the bread is soft and can be used as a pancake. To make the characteristically crisp *carasau* bread, replace the sheets separately in the oven until they are dry and crunchy (about 5 minutes). Cool on a wire rack.

grissini

THESE ITALIAN BREADSTICKS CAN BE SERVED WITH APPETIZERS, WITH DIPS, OR AS A CANAPÉ—AND BABIES LOVE THEM.
YOU CAN COAT THEM TO YOUR TASTE WITH COARSE SALT, WITH SESAME OR FENNEL SEEDS, OR WITH DRIED HERBS.
TO MAKE THESE COATINGS STICK, BRUSH THE BREADSTICKS WITH EGG GLAZE BEFORE BAKING THEM.

    I ONCE WENT TO A DINNER PARTY FOR WHICH THE FIRST-NAME INITIAL OF EVERY GUEST HAD BEEN BAKED FROM
BREADSTICK DOUGH. THE INITIALS WERE THEN PRESENTED ON WHITE NAPKINS. THEY LOOKED WONDERFUL.

1 Sift the flour and salt into a large bowl and make a well in the center. In a separate small bowl, cream the yeast and sugar with 1 tbsp of the water. Add the yeast mixture and oil to the well in the flour, together with enough of the remaining water to make a firm, sticky dough.

2 Tip the dough out onto a well-floured surface and knead it for 10 minutes, until it is smooth and elastic. Cover with a damp dish towel, and leave to rest for 10 minutes.

3 Punch down and knead the dough for a further 10 minutes on a lightly floured surface. Shape into a 12 x 8-inch rectangle that is about three-quarters of an inch thick. Cover it again with the dish towel and leave to rest for a further 10 minutes.

4 Preheat the oven to 400°F. Lightly oil two baking sheets and sprinkle them with the semolina.

5 Cut the dough rectangle widthwise into four equal pieces, then cut each of these pieces into 10 strips. Stretch each strip until it is about 10 inches long, then roll on a flour-free surface into rounded sticks (they would slip on a floured surface). Place them well apart on the baking sheets.

6 Bake for 15-20 minutes. Transfer to a wire rack and leave to cool and become crisp.

18OZ OR 3⅗ CUPS (500G) WHITE BREAD FLOUR

2 TSP FINE SEA SALT

½OZ (15G) FRESH YEAST

½ TSP GRANULATED SUGAR

9FL OZ OR 1⅛ CUPS (250ML) WATER AT BODY TEMPERATURE

3 TBSP OLIVE OIL

2 TBSP FINE SEMOLINA

tomato and basil fougasse

THIS CLASSIC FLATTISH BREAD FROM PROVENCE IN SOUTHERN FRANCE CAN BE MADE PLAIN OR FLAVORED—FOR INSTANCE, WITH CHEESE, SPICES, OR HERBS. I HAVE CHOSEN TO ADD INGREDIENTS HERE: SOME BASIL AND TOMATO, WHICH WORK WELL TOGETHER. YOU CAN OF COURSE LEAVE THEM OUT.

1LB OR 3⅗ CUPS (450G) WHITE BREAD FLOUR

1 TSP FINE SEA SALT

¾OZ (20G) FRESH YEAST, CRUMBLED

9FL OZ OR 1⅛ CUPS (290ML) WATER AT
    BODY TEMPERATURE

OLIVE OIL

4OZ (115G) SMALL CHERRY TOMATOES, CHOPPED

A HANDFUL OF FRESH BASIL LEAVES,
    ROUGHLY CHOPPED

1 Put the flour and salt into a large bowl and make a well in the center. Cream the yeast with 1 tbsp of the water, then add it to the well in the flour with 1 tbsp of the olive oil and the remaining water. Mix until the dough comes away from the sides of the bowl.

2 Knead the dough on a lightly floured surface for about 10 minutes. Place it in a lightly oiled bowl, cover with a damp dish towel, and leave to rise for 1 hour.

3 Punch down the dough, then turn it out onto a lightly floured surface and knead for 5 minutes. Divide the dough into two equal pieces and flatten them. Sprinkle the tomatoes and basil over them and fold each piece of dough several times to incorporate the tomatoes and basil evenly.

4 Shape each piece of dough into an oblong about 11 x 6 inches in size. Using a sharp knife, make four diagonal cuts into the interior of each loaf and pull the cuts apart slightly to make a ladder effect. Place onto a lightly oiled baking sheet, cover with a damp dish towel, and leave to proof for 1 hour, or until the dough has doubled in size.

5 Preheat the oven to 425°F.

6 Drizzle each loaf with olive oil and bake for 25 minutes, until they are golden. Cool on a wire rack.

rustic walnut bread

I LOVE THIS CLASSIC WALNUT BREAD, PARTICULARLY IF IT IS SERVED WITH A STRONG CHEESE. THE COMBINATION IS VERY GOOD, BUT THE WALNUTS MUST BE FRESH. THE BREAD IS EXCELLENT FOR SANDWICHES OR FOR MOPPING UP THE JUICES FROM A GRATIN OR THE DRESSING FROM A SALAD.

1LB 5OZ OR 4⅘ CUPS (600G) WHITE BREAD FLOUR

1 TSP FINE SEA SALT

1OZ OR 2 TBSP (25G) UNSALTED BUTTER, SOFTENED
   AND DICED

1 TSP FENNEL SEEDS, CRUSHED

4OZ OR APPROXIMATELY 1 CUP (120G) ROUGHLY
   CHOPPED FRESH WALNUT PIECES

½OZ (15G) FRESH YEAST, CRUMBLED

12FL OZ OR 1½ CUPS (350ML) WATER AT
   BODY TEMPERATURE

1 Sift the flour and salt into a large warmed mixing bowl. Rub in the butter until the mixture resembles bread crumbs. Stir in the fennel seeds and walnuts and make a well in the center. Cream the fresh yeast and 2 tbsp of the water. Add this to the well in the flour and, using a wooden spoon, add as much of the remaining water as necessary to mix to a smooth ball of dough.

2 Turn the dough out onto a lightly floured work surface and knead for 10 minutes, until it is smooth. Divide the dough into two pieces. Shape each into a round and place on an oiled baking tray. Cover with a damp dish towel and leave to rise for about 1 hour, until doubled in size.

3 Preheat the oven to 425°F.

4 Punch down the dough, then knead it for 2–3 minutes on a lightly floured surface. Reshape, cover with the dish towel, and leave to proof for 20 minutes.

5 Slash the tops of each round with a sharp knife and bake for 10 minutes. Reduce the temperature to 375°F and bake for a further 20 minutes, until the bread sounds hollow when tapped on the bottom with your fingertips. If the bread starts becoming too dark while cooking, cover it loosely with foil. Cool on a wire rack.

variation
You could make a single loaf from this dough. It will take 1½ hours to rise, 10 minutes to proof, and 40 minutes to bake.

pita bread

THIS IS THE STAPLE BREAD OF THE MIDDLE EAST, MOST COMMONLY KNOWN IN THE WEST BY ITS GREEK NAME, PITA.
IT IS A FLATBREAD IN ESSENCE BUT IT IS ALSO A CLASSIC, WHICH IS WHY IT IS INCLUDED HERE IN THIS CHAPTER. IT CAN
BE EATEN WITH DIPS, USED AS A SCOOP, OR SPLIT AND USED AS A WRAP.

9OZ OR 1⅘ CUPS (250G) WHITE BREAD FLOUR

9OZ OR 2 CUPS + 2TSP (250G)
    WHOLE-WHEAT FLOUR

1 TSP FINE SEA SALT

½OZ (15G) FRESH YEAST, CRUMBLED

½ TSP GRANULATED SUGAR

10FL OZ OR 1¼ CUPS (300ML) WATER AT
    BODY TEMPERATURE

2 TBSP OLIVE OIL

1 Sift the flours and the salt into a large bowl. Some grains from the whole-wheat flour will be caught in the sifter or sieve; tip them into the bowl and make a well in the center. In a separate small bowl, cream the yeast and sugar with 1 tbsp of the water. Add the yeast mixture and olive oil to the well in the flour, with enough of the water to make a firm but soft dough.

2 Tip the dough out onto a lightly floured work surface and knead until it is smooth, supple, and elastic: about 15 minutes. It will be quite stiff at first but will stretch and become easier to work after a few minutes. Place it in a lightly oiled bowl, turn to coat evenly with oil, then cover with a damp dish towel and leave to rise for about 1½ hours, until it has doubled in size.

3 Punch down the dough, knead for 2–3 minutes, then rest, covered, for 10 minutes.

4 Divide the dough into eight pieces and shape each into a ball. Roll out on a lightly floured work surface to the characteristic pita oval, about 9 inches long and a quarter-inch thick. Cover with the dish towel again and leave to proof for about 20 minutes.

5 Preheat the oven to 425°F. Dust two baking sheets lightly with flour and preheat in the oven for 5 minutes.

6 Place the ovals of bread on the two hot baking sheets and return them to the oven immediately. Bake for 5–10 minutes, until the breads puff up. Wrap in a clean, dry cloth to keep the crusts soft, because the breads can dry out fairly quickly.

sourdough bread

FOR ME, THIS BREAD DOUGH—INSPIRED BY ONE IN THE USA—IS THE ULTIMATE FOR FLAVOR, AND ALTHOUGH IT DOES TAKE TIME, IT IS WELL WORTH IT. AT THE CORDON VERT COOKERY SCHOOL IN ENGLAND, WHERE I TEACH, IT HAS BEEN VOTED THE BEST BREAD, AND ONCE THE STUDENTS HAVE TRIED IT THEY ARE ALL CONVERTED. I HOPE YOU WILL BE, TOO. IT ISN'T VERY FAST, I ADMIT, BECAUSE OF THE *BIGA* (WHICH I USE INSTEAD OF THE REALLY TRADITIONAL SOURDOUGH STARTER), BUT THE INDIVIDUAL STAGES DON'T TAKE ALL THAT LONG. TRY TO FIT THESE STAGES INTO THE RHYTHM OF YOUR DAY AND THE WONDERFUL BREAD THAT RESULTS WON'T SEEM AT ALL SLOW...

¼OZ (10G) FRESH YEAST, CRUMBLED

8FL OZ OR 1 CUP (ABOUT 225ML) WATER
    AT BODY TEMPERATURE

18OZ OR 3⅗ CUPS (500G) WHITE BREAD FLOUR

½ RECIPE *BIGA* (*SEE* PAGE 12)

½ TBSP FINE SEA SALT

1 Dissolve the yeast in 2fl oz or ¼ cup (50ml) of the water and add this and 3oz or ⅗ cup (85g) of the flour to the *biga*. Mix well. The mixture should be slack; if it is not, add a little more water. Leave for a further 24 hours.

2 The following day, add the salt and the remaining water and flour and mix together. Knead well for 10 minutes, adding more flour if necessary. Put the dough in a bowl, cover with a damp dish towel, and leave to rise in a warm place for 1 hour, until it has doubled in size.

3 Punch down and knead the dough for 2-3 minutes on a lightly floured surface. Cover with a damp dish towel and leave to rise again for a further hour.

4 Punch down for a second time. Knead for 3 minutes on a lightly floured surface, then shape into a large oval. Place on a baking sheet, slash the top three times, and dust with flour. Cover and leave to proof for 15 minutes.

5 Preheat the oven to 400°F.

6 Place a roasting pan containing a little water in the bottom of the oven; 4 tbsp should be plenty, unless it evaporates (*see* page 26 on steam). Bake the bread for 25-30 minutes, until it is golden brown and sounds hollow when tapped with your fingertips. Cool on a wire rack.

chocolate brioche

THIS A FAIL-SAFE RECIPE—ONE THAT I'VE USED FOR YEARS. PEOPLE ARE OFTEN PUT OFF BY BRIOCHE, THINKING IT DIFFICULT AND TIME-CONSUMING, BUT IT CAN BE FAST AND EASY. THE CHOCOLATE ISN'T NECESSARY, BUT IT IS A NICE TOUCH AND IS A GREAT OCCASIONAL TREAT FOR CHILDREN.

1 Sift the flour into a large bowl with the salt and sugar and make a well in the center. Dissolve the yeast in the water, then add it to the well in the flour along with the beaten eggs and milk. Stir until you have a soft dough.

2 Turn the dough out onto a lightly floured board and knead it for 5 minutes. Add the butter a few pieces at a time; don't add the next piece until you have incorporated the first. Wrap the dough in plastic wrap and refrigerate for 1 hour (or you could leave it in the fridge overnight).

3 Grease 12 small brioche pans (these have fluted edges, rather like small cupcake paper cases). Punch down and knead the dough on a lightly floured surface for 2-3 minutes. Divide it into 12 pieces and shape each into a smooth round. Place a square of chocolate in the center of each

and bring up the sides of the dough. Press the edges together to seal them. Place the brioches, seam-side down, in the prepared pans, cover, and leave in a warm place to proof until they have doubled in size: about 20 minutes.

4 Preheat the oven to 400°F.

5 Brush the tops of the brioches with beaten egg to glaze, then bake for 12-15 minutes. Cool slightly, then, while they are still warm, drizzle with extra melted chocolate. Serve.

variation
You could, of course, make plain brioche, either as one large loaf or as small loaves as above. Add a little vanilla extract to the dough first. For the large brioche, proof the dough for about 40 minutes and bake it in a 1lb loaf pan or a large brioche pan for 45 minutes. You could also bake it as a plaited loaf on a greased baking sheet.

DOUGH

9OZ OR 1⅘ CUPS (250G) WHITE BREAD FLOUR

A PINCH OF FINE SEA SALT

2 TBSP SUPERFINE SUGAR

¼OZ (10G) FRESH YEAST, CRUMBLED

1 TBSP WATER AT BODY TEMPERATURE

3 LARGE EGGS, BEATEN

4 TBSP MILK AT BODY TEMPERATURE

4OZ OR 8 TBSP (115G) UNSALTED BUTTER, DICED, AT ROOM TEMPERATURE

6OZ (175G) DARK CHOCOLATE, IN SQUARES

GLAZE AND FINISH

1 LARGE EGG, BEATEN

A LITTLE EXTRA DARK CHOCOLATE, MELTED

rolls and buns

ROLLS AND BUNS TAKE A MUCH SHORTER TIME TO RISE, PROOF, AND BAKE THAN LOAVES DO. BREAD CANNOT BE CONJURED UP IN A MINUTE; FOR THE BEST FLAVORS AND TEXTURES, TIME IS INEVITABLY INVOLVED. YET IF YOU DIMINISH THE SIZE OF THE DOUGH TO BE RISEN, PROOFED, AND BAKED, YOU LESSEN THE TIME INVOLVED IN THE ENTIRE PROCESS. OF COURSE, ALL THE DOUGHS HERE CAN BE MADE INTO LOAVES OF WHATEVER SHAPE YOU LIKE; THEY WILL JUST TAKE MUCH LONGER.

I LIKE TO THINK OF ROLLS AND BUNS AS THE "FUN BREADS:" GREAT FOR SNACKS, PARTIES, ENTERTAINING, PICNICS, OR TRAVELING IN THE CAR. THEY PACK EASILY, THEY CAN CONTAIN EXTRA FILLINGS, AND BECAUSE THEY ARE INDIVIDUAL,

THEY ALWAYS HAVE THAT ELEMENT OF BEING SOMETHING SPECIAL. CHILDREN CAN HELP MAKE ROLLS AND BUNS, AND THEY LIKE TO EAT THEM, TOO. MY DAUGHTER ANTONIA LOVES THE LITTLE ROLLS I MAKE FOR HER; I THINK IT'S BECAUSE OF THE ELEMENT OF SURPRISE.

IN THIS CHAPTER WE HAVE SAVORY AND SWEET, SOME CLASSIC, AND SOME SLIGHTLY MORE EXOTIC RECIPES. ALL HAVE BEEN DESIGNED TO FIT INTO OUR INCREASINGLY BUSY LIVES, AND I HOPE THEY INSPIRE YOU TO BAKE AND CREATE EVEN MORE INTERESTING COMBINATIONS.

anchovy rolls

THESE WONDERFULLY CRISP ROLLS FEATURE EVERY SPRING IN AGRIGENTO'S WHEAT-FESTIVAL CELEBRATIONS IN SICILY. THEY ARE HAND-CRAFTED BY THE WOMEN OF THE TOWN AND FRIED IN HUGE VATS OF OIL. I HAVE MODIFIED THE RECIPE A LITTLE, AND YOU CAN USE OTHER FILLINGS SUCH AS MOZZARELLA, OLIVES, AND ANCHOVIES, OR HERBS AND CHEESE. THEY ARE GREAT WITH SOUPS AND SALADS, FOR PICNICS, OR AS CANAPÉS—AND CHILDREN LOVE THEM, TOO.

DOUGH

9OZ OR 1⅘ CUPS (250G) WHITE BREAD FLOUR

2 TSP FINE SEA SALT

OLIVE OIL

¼OZ (10G) FRESH YEAST, CRUMBLED

5FL OZ OR ⅝ CUP (150ML) WATER AT
    BODY TEMPERATURE

FILLING

16 ANCHOVIES

1 In a large bowl, mix the flour and salt together. Make a well in the center and add 2 tbsp of the oil. Dissolve the yeast in a third of the water and add to the well in the flour. Using a wooden spoon, add enough of the remaining water to form a firm but damp dough.

2 Turn the dough out onto a lightly floured surface and knead for about 10 minutes. Place in a lightly oiled bowl, cover with a damp dish towel, and leave to rise for 1 hour.

3 After 1 hour, punch down the dough and knead again for 5 minutes to relax it. Cover and leave to rest for another 5 minutes.

4 Divide the rested dough into 16 little balls. Flatten each in the palm of your hand, fill it with an anchovy, and pinch it closed into a ball, enclosing the filling. Put the little balls on a greased baking tray, seam-side down, cover, and leave to proof for 25 minutes.

5 Preheat the oven to 400°F.

6 Bake the rolls for 12–15 minutes, until they are golden. Cool on a wire rack and eat while still warm.

cheese and onion crown rolls

THESE ROLLS ARE FILLING AND DELICIOUS FOR PICNICS OR FOR THE CHILDREN'S LUNCH BOXES. THE DOUGH CAN ALSO BE BAKED AS ONE LARGE LOAF (*SEE* VARIATION BELOW).

1 TBSP OLIVE OIL

1 RED ONION, PEELED AND FINELY SLICED

2OZ OR 4 TBSP (55G) UNSALTED BUTTER

3½FL OZ OR 7 TBSP (100ML) MILK

½OZ (15G) FRESH YEAST, CRUMBLED

½ TSP SUPERFINE SUGAR

2 LARGE EGGS, BEATEN

8OZ OR 2 CUPS (225G) WHOLE-WHEAT FLOUR

1 TSP FINE SEA SALT

4OZ OR ABOUT 1 CUP (115G) GRUYÈRE CHEESE, FRESHLY GRATED (USE CHEDDAR IF UNAVAILABLE)

1 Heat the oil in a saucepan. Add the onion and cook gently for 4-5 minutes, until it is soft but not colored.

2 Melt the butter in the milk and, when it is up to body temperature, mix with the yeast, sugar, and eggs.

3 Put the flour and salt in a large bowl and make a well in the center. Pour in the yeast mixture and mix to a smooth dough.

4 Tip out onto a lightly floured work surface and knead for 10 minutes. Place in a lightly oiled bowl, cover with a damp dish towel, and leave to rise for 1 hour, or until the dough has doubled in size.

5 Preheat the oven to 425°F. Lightly oil an 8-inch round cake pan.

6 Punch down the dough, then turn it out onto a floured work surface and knead or chafe in the onions and three-quarters of the cheese. Divide the dough into six rolls and place in the cake pan. Leave to proof, covered with a damp dish towel, for 20-30 minutes, until doubled in size.

7 Bake the rolls for 20-30 minutes. Remove them from the oven, brush with a little extra milk, and sprinkle with the remaining cheese. Bake for a further 5 minutes. Leave the rolls to become cold in the pan on a wire rack before separating them.

variation

Make this dough into a free-form bread on a baking sheet—you can make it round, square, oval, or long—or put it in a 1lb loaf pan. Bake it for 30-40 minutes.

cheese and potato rolls

THESE LOVELY, CRUSTY ROLLS ARE A GREAT ACCOMPANIMENT TO ANY GOOD HOMEMADE SOUP. THE DOUGH CAN ALSO BE USED TO MAKE A FANTASTIC LARGE LOAF (*SEE* VARIATION BELOW).

1 Mash the potatoes with the milk and soft goat cheese. Sift the flour into a bowl with the salt and make a well in the center. Dissolve the yeast in 2 tbsp of the water and add to the well in the flour. Add the potato mixture and gradually mix in enough of the remaining water to make a soft dough.

2 Tip the dough out onto a lightly floured surface and knead for 10-15 minutes until it is smooth and elastic. Leave it to rise in a lightly oiled bowl, covered with a damp dish towel, for 1 hour, until it has doubled in size.

3 Preheat the oven to 425°F.

4 Punch down the dough, then knead it again for about 2-3 minutes. Shape it into about 16 round rolls and make a cross on each with a sharp knife. Place them, spaced apart, on a greased baking sheet and lightly dust with extra flour. Cover and leave to proof for 15-20 minutes.

5 Bake the rolls for 10 minutes, then turn the oven down to 375°F. Bake for a further 15 minutes, until the rolls are golden and the base sounds hollow when tapped with the fingertips. Cool on a wire rack.

variation

For a single loaf, place the dough in a greased 2lb loaf pan, then bake for 10 minutes, followed by a further 30 minutes at the lower temperature.

1LB (450G) OLD POTATOES, PEELED AND FRESHLY BOILED UNTIL TENDER

5FL OZ OR ⅝ CUP (150ML) MILK

3½OZ OR A GENEROUS ⅓ CUP (100G) SOFT GOAT CHEESE

1½LB OR 4⅘ CUPS (675G) WHITE BREAD FLOUR

2 TSP FINE SEA SALT

1OZ (25G) FRESH YEAST, CRUMBLED

15FL OZ OR 1⅞ CUPS (425ML) WATER AT BODY TEMPERATURE

camembert and wild mushroom rolls

THESE ROLLS ARE GREAT BATCH-BAKED IN A NEAT CIRCLE. THE WHOLE CIRCLE IS EASILY TRANSPORTED IN A PICNIC BASKET, AND EVERYBODY TEARS OFF HIS OR HER OWN SOFT, ALREADY-FILLED ROLLS!

8OZ OR 1⅗ CUPS (225G) WHITE BREAD FLOUR

8OZ OR 2 CUPS (225G) WHOLE-WHEAT FLOUR

1 TBSP FINE SEA SALT

2OZ OR 4 TBSP (55G) UNSALTED BUTTER, SOFTENED AND DICED

1OZ (25G) FRESH YEAST, CRUMBLED

10FL OZ OR 1¼ CUPS (300ML) WATER AT BODY TEMPERATURE

4½OZ (125G) WILD MUSHROOMS, SOAKED IF USING DRIED, ROUGHLY CHOPPED

4½OZ OR ABOUT ½ CUP (125G) CAMEMBERT CHEESE, DICED (USE BRIE IF UNAVAILABLE)

1 Put the flours and salt into a large bowl. Rub in the butter until the mixture resembles bread crumbs, then make a well in the center. Dissolve the yeast in 2 tbsp of the water and add to the well in the flour. Mix in, adding enough of the remaining water to make a smooth dough.

2 On a lightly floured surface, knead the dough for 5 minutes until it is smooth and elastic. Place it in a lightly oiled bowl, cover with a damp dish towel, and leave to rise for 1 hour, until it has doubled in size.

3 Punch down the dough, then tip it out onto a lightly floured surface and knead for 2–3 minutes. Cut it into 12 even pieces. Roll each piece slightly and place 1 tsp of the mushrooms in the center with 1 tbsp of Camembert. Carefully wrap the dough around

the filling and place the rolls, spaced apart and seam-side down, on a greased baking sheet. Cover with the dish towel and leave to proof for 20–25 minutes, until they have doubled in size.

4 Preheat the oven to 400°F.

5 Dust the rolls with extra flour and bake for 10–15 minutes, until they are risen and golden. Cool on a wire rack.

variation

To make a single loaf, roll the dough out to a rectangle of about 14 x 8 inches. Cover with the mushrooms and Camembert and roll up like a Swiss roll, from the long side. Make several holes (with a skewer or similar) through the dough, place it on an oiled baking sheet, and bake it for 35 minutes.

brie and bacon mini-loaves

THESE MINI-LOAVES OF BREAD ARE DELIGHTFUL IF EATEN WHEN THEY ARE STILL SLIGHTLY WARM, SO THAT THE BRIE IS STILL SOFT, BUT THEY ARE EQUALLY GREAT COLD FOR A PICNIC.

1 Put the flour and salt into a large bowl, and rub in the butter until the mixture resembles fine bread crumbs. Cream the yeast with 2 tbsp of the milk in a small bowl. Make a well in the center of the flour, and add the yeast liquid, eggs, and enough of the remaining milk to make a soft dough.

2 Tip the dough out onto a lightly floured surface and knead for 5 minutes, until it is smooth and elastic. Place in a lightly oiled bowl, cover with a damp dish towel, and leave to rise for 1 hour, until it has doubled in size.

3 Punch down the dough, then tip it out onto a lightly floured surface and knead for 2-3 minutes. Cut into six pieces. Roll one piece of dough at a time to a 3 x 4-inch rectangle. Place a slice of Brie in the center with a teaspoon-sized piece of bacon.

Wrap the dough around the filling (fold the short ends in first, then the long ends), then place in a greased 4 x 2¼ x 1½-inch mini-loaf pan, seam-side down. Repeat to fill six pans.

4 Place the loaf pans on a baking sheet, cover the top with a clean dish towel, and leave to proof for 1 hour, until it has doubled in size.

5 Preheat the oven to 400°F.

6 Bake the mini-loaves for 12-15 minutes, until they are golden and the base of each sounds hollow when tapped with the fingertips. Carefully loosen the loaves from the pans using a sharp knife and allow to cool slightly on a wire rack.

9OZ OR 1⅘ CUPS (250G) WHITE BREAD FLOUR

¼ TSP FINE SEA SALT

3OZ OR 6 TBSP (85G) UNSALTED BUTTER, SOFTENED

1OZ (25G) FRESH YEAST, CRUMBLED

3 TBSP WARM MILK

2 LARGE EGGS, BEATEN

2OZ (55G) BRIE DE MEAUX CHEESE, CUT INTO 6 SLICES

2OZ (55G) BACON OR PANCETTA, PRE-FRIED

anchovy cloverleaf rolls

THIS IS A PROVENÇAL RECIPE AND THE ROLLS ARE DELICIOUS SERVED WITH A *SALADE NIÇOISE*. THEIR SLIGHTLY SALTY AND POWERFUL FLAVOR MAKES THEM A GREAT ACCOMPANIMENT FOR ANY LIGHT, LEAFY SALAD.

1 Sift the flour and salt into a large bowl. Rub in the butter until the mixture resembles bread crumbs and make a well in the center. Cream the yeast with 1 tbsp of the water, then add to the well in the flour, along with the eggs, brandy, and enough of the remaining water to make a smooth dough.

2 On a lightly floured work surface, knead the dough for 5 minutes, until it is smooth and elastic. Place in a lightly oiled bowl, cover with a damp dish towel, and leave to rise for 45 minutes, or until it has doubled in size.

3 Punch down and then tip the dough onto a lightly floured work surface and knead in 10 of the chopped anchovies (reserve the remaining five for the topping). Divide the dough into 12 even pieces. Split each piece into three

balls and place together in a cloverleaf shape on a greased baking sheet. Cover and leave to proof for 15-20 minutes, until doubled in size.

4 Preheat the oven to 400°F.

5 Brush the top of each roll with beaten egg to glaze, and sprinkle with the reserved anchovies. Bake for 12-15 minutes, until golden. Cool on a wire rack.

variation

To make one large loaf, still in the cloverleaf shape, divide the dough into three and roll into balls. Arrange in a cloverleaf shape on an oiled baking sheet and bake for 25-35 minutes.

DOUGH

18OZ OR 3⅗ CUPS (500G) WHITE BREAD FLOUR

½ TSP FINE SEA SALT

2OZ OR 4 TBSP (55G) UNSALTED BUTTER, SOFTENED AND DICED

1OZ (25G) FRESH YEAST, CRUMBLED

5FL OZ OR ⅝ CUP (150ML) WATER AT BODY TEMPERATURE

2 LARGE EGGS, BEATEN

2 TBSP BRANDY

15 SALTED ANCHOVIES, RINSED AND FINELY CHOPPED

GLAZE

1 LARGE EGG, BEATEN

french potato bread rolls

THESE LITTLE ROLLS ARE PARTICULARLY GOOD SERVED WITH CHEESE, OR TOPPED WITH CHEESE AS AN ACCOMPANIMENT TO A SUBSTANTIAL SOUP. THEY ARE VERY VERSATILE AND CAN ALSO BE BAKED AS A TOPPING FOR A STEW, SAY, OR USED TO PROVIDE A BASE FOR TOPPINGS, OR THE DOUGH CAN BE BAKED INTO ONE LOAF (*SEE* VARIATION BELOW).

18OZ OR 3⅗ CUPS (500G) WHITE BREAD FLOUR

1 TSP FINE SEA SALT

8OZ OR ABOUT 1 CUP (225G) WARM MASHED POTATO

½OZ (15G) FRESH YEAST, CRUMBLED

10FL OZ OR 1¼ CUPS (300ML) MILK AND WATER IN EQUAL QUANTITIES, AT BODY TEMPERATURE

1 Sift the flour and salt together into a large bowl. Rub the potato into the flour as if rubbing in butter, to make a smooth mixture, and make a well in the center. Dissolve the yeast in a little of the liquid and add to the well in the flour. Using a wooden spoon, mix in enough of the remaining liquid to make a smooth dough.

2 Tip the dough out onto a lightly floured surface and knead it for 5 minutes until smooth and elastic. Leave to rise for 40 minutes in a lightly oiled bowl covered with a damp dish towel until it has doubled in size.

3 Preheat the oven to 425°F. Flour a baking sheet.

4 Knead the dough once more and divide into 12 equal pieces. Shape into bread rolls and place them, spaced apart, on the floured baking sheet. Cover lightly with a damp dish towel and leave to proof for 15-20 minutes, until they have doubled in size. Dust them lightly with flour.

5 Bake for 12-15 minutes, or until they are risen and golden. Cool on a wire rack.

variation

You can make this dough into one large loaf in a 2lb loaf pan. Bake for 25-30 minutes, perhaps with some seeds on top.

butternut squash bread rolls

THIS IS A GOOD BREAD FOR AUTUMN, WHEN SQUASHES ARE AT THEIR BEST, AND IT CAN ALSO BE SERVED WITH A LENTIL SOUP FOR TRADITIONAL ITALIAN NEW YEAR'S EVE FARE. THE LENTILS SIGNIFY THAT THE NEW YEAR WILL BRING MONEY.

1 Put half of the flour on the work surface and make a well in the center. Heat the milk until just warm, then cream the yeast in a little of it. Add the yeast liquid to the well in the flour, along with the remaining milk, and mix to a dough.

2 Knead the dough for 10 minutes, until it is smooth. Put it into an oiled bowl, cover with a damp dish towel, and leave to rise for 1 hour.

3 Meanwhile, preheat the oven to 400°F and oil a baking sheet. Bake the squash for 20 minutes, until it is soft. Purée the squash with a masher, then mix in the raisins. Allow it to cool before adding it to the dough.

4 Punch down the dough. Add the squash and raisins to the dough with the remaining flour on a lightly floured work surface, and knead well for 10 minutes. Return to the oiled bowl, cover with a damp dish towel, and leave to rise for a further hour.

5 Preheat the oven to 400°F. Lightly butter a baking sheet.

6 Divide the dough into five pieces. Form each into a slightly flat circle and arrange the circles about 2-3 inches apart on the buttered baking tray. Cover with the dish towel and leave to proof for a further 10 minutes.

7 Bake the rolls for 25 minutes, during which time they will join up into a flat loaf. Remove from the oven and cool a little on a wire rack before breaking into rolls and then pieces.

10½OZ OR 2 CUPS + 1 TBSP (300G) WHITE
    BREAD FLOUR

3½FL OZ OR ⅜ CUP + 1 TBSP (100ML) WHOLE MILK

¼OZ (10G) FRESH YEAST, CRUMBLED

9OZ (250G) BUTTERNUT SQUASH, PEELED,
    DESEEDED, AND FINELY DICED

2¾OZ OR ABOUT ½ CUP (75G) RAISINS,
    SOAKED IN WARM WATER FOR 20 MINUTES
    AND SQUEEZED DRY

OLIVE OIL

UNSALTED BUTTER

BIGA: 8–12 hours   **RISING:** 3 hours   **PROOFING:** 15 minutes   **BAKING:** 15–20 minutes   **DRIED YEAST:** ½ tsp (*biga*) and 2 tsp (dough)

MAKES: 12 rolls

slipper bread rolls

CIABATTA'S ORIGINS LIE IN EMILIA-ROMAGNA, THE GASTRONOMIC CENTER OF ITALY. IT IS A RECIPE THAT I AM CONSTANTLY HONING, BUT I AM NOW TRULY HAPPY WITH THE RESULTS. IF YOU DO THE VARIOUS STAGES AT TIMES CONVENIENT TO YOU, IT WON'T TAKE VERY LONG.

CIABATTA BIGA

9OZ OR 1⅘ CUPS (250G) WHITE BREAD FLOUR

⅛OZ (5G) FRESH YEAST, CRUMBLED

5FL OZ OR ⅝ CUP (150ML) WATER AT
    BODY TEMPERATURE

CIABATTA DOUGH

10FL OZ OR 1¼ CUPS (300ML) WATER AT
    BODY TEMPERATURE

½OZ (15G) FRESH YEAST, CRUMBLED

18OZ OR 3⅗ CUPS (500G) WHITE BREAD FLOUR

2 TSP FINE SEA SALT

4 TBSP OLIVE OIL

1 Start with the *biga*. Put the flour in a large bowl and make a well in the center. Dissolve the yeast in 1 tbsp of the water and add it to the well with enough of the remaining water to mix it to a slack dough.

2 Knead it on a work surface for 2 minutes, return it to the bowl, cover with a damp dish towel, and leave at room temperature for 8–12 hours. It will rise and then fall.

3 The next day, put the water for the *ciabatta* in a jug or bowl and crumble in the yeast. Mix well, then add it to the *biga*. Stir and squeeze with your fingers to make a thick, smooth dough. Work in half the flour to make a very sticky dough and beat it with your hands for 5 minutes, until it is well stretched and elastic. Cover the bowl with a damp dish towel and leave to rise in a warm place until it has doubled in size: about 2 hours.

4 Add the salt and oil to the dough, then gradually work in the rest of the flour to make a soft, sticky dough. Carry on kneading until it is smooth and very elastic, cover with a damp dish towel, and leave to rise in a warm place until it has doubled in size: about 1 hour.

5 Meanwhile, preheat the oven to 400°F, and gently warm a baking sheet.

6 Carefully tip the dough onto a well-floured work surface. Using a well-floured bread scraper or palette knife, divide it into 12 pieces. Don't make them uniform; odd shapes add charm. Dust with flour, then cover with a damp dish towel and leave to proof for 15 minutes.

7 Punch down the rolls slightly, dimpling them with your thumb, then bake for 15–20 minutes, until they are golden brown and crisp.

variation

To make two slipper-shaped loaves, proof the dough for 30 minutes and then bake for 25–30 minutes.

semolina bread rolls

THESE ROLLS ARE FROM PUGLIA IN SOUTHERN ITALY AND ARE IDEAL FOR BREAKFAST. SEMOLINA IMPARTS COLOR AND A LIGHTLY GRAINY TEXTURE AND CRUST. FLAVOR THE DOUGH WITH A HANDFUL OF CHOPPED FRESH HERBS—OR A SPRINKLING OF DRIED—IF YOU WANT TO.

1 Place the flour, semolina flour, and black pepper on a work surface, pile into a mound, and make a well in the center. Dissolve the yeast in 2 tbsp of the water, then add this and the *biga* to the well in the flour, along with the remaining water. Mix with your hands until all the ingredients are well combined, which will take about 5 minutes.

2 Add the fine salt and knead the dough for 10 minutes, until it is smooth and elastic. Do the stretch test to check that the dough is ready (*see* page 18). Place the dough in a large, lightly oiled bowl, cover with a damp dish towel, and leave in a warm place until it has doubled in size: approximately 1½ hours.

3 Punch down the dough, knead for 2–3 minutes on a lightly floured surface, then cover and leave to rise again for 30 minutes. This second rising will give the dough more strength.

4 Tip the dough onto a lightly floured surface and cut into 12 pieces, using a dough scraper or sharp knife. Shape into balls, place on a lightly oiled baking tray, and leave to proof for half an hour.

5 Preheat the oven to 400°F.

6 Using a sharp knife, cut a cross on top of each roll, then sprinkle liberally with coarse salt. Bake in the preheated oven for 20 minutes, opening the oven door slightly for the last 5 to make the rolls crisper. Cool on a wire rack and eat warm.

13OZ OR 2⅗ CUPS (375G) WHITE BREAD FLOUR

10OZ OR 1⅔ CUPS (275G) FINE SEMOLINA FLOUR

2 TSP COARSELY GROUND BLACK PEPPER

¼OZ (10G) FRESH YEAST, CRUMBLED

13FL OZ OR 1⅝ CUPS (375ML) WATER AT BODY TEMPERATURE

1 RECIPE *BIGA* (*SEE* PAGE 12)

½OZ (15G) FINE SEA SALT

OLIVE OIL

2 TBSP COARSE SEA SALT

RISING: 1 hour **PROOFING:** 1 hour **BAKING:** 15 minutes **DRIED YEAST:** 2½ tsp **MAKES:** 12 buns

hot cross buns

THESE BUNS ARE TRADITIONAL AT EASTER BUT ARE GREAT AT ANY TIME OF YEAR, ESPECIALLY IN WINTER, WHEN ALL THEIR SPICES CONJURE UP IMAGES OF COMFORT AND WARMTH IN FRONT OF THE FIRE. THEY ARE DELICIOUS SPLIT AND TOASTED, WITH LOADS OF BUTTER—AND JAM, IF YOU WISH.

1 Sift the flour into a large bowl, add the butter, and rub it in with your fingertips until the mixture resembles fine bread crumbs. Stir in the sugar, salt, and spices and make a well in the center. Blend the yeast with 2 tbsp of the milk in a small bowl and add to the well in the flour, together with the egg and enough of the remaining milk to form a smooth dough.

2 Knead the dough for 5 minutes on a lightly floured work surface until it is smooth and elastic. Gradually incorporate the raisins, sultanas, and candied peel. Place the dough in a lightly oiled bowl, cover with a damp dish towel, and leave to rise for 1 hour, or until it has doubled in size.

3 Punch down the dough, then tip it out onto a lightly floured surface and knead for 2–3 minutes.

Cut it into 12 even pieces and shape into balls. Place on a greased baking sheet, spaced well apart. Cover with a damp dish towel and leave to proof for an hour, until it has doubled in size.

4 Preheat the oven to 400°F.

5 Mix the water, flour, and egg in a bowl to make a paste for the crosses. Pour into a small plastic bag and tie a knot in the top. Snip the corner of the bag. Pipe crosses onto each bun.

6 Bake the buns for 15 minutes, until they are golden. While they are still warm, brush them with golden syrup. Cool on a wire rack.

DOUGH

1LB OR 3⅕ CUPS (450G) WHITE BREAD FLOUR

6 TBSP UNSALTED BUTTER, SOFTENED AND DICED

3OZ OR ½ CUP (85G) SOFT LIGHT BROWN SUGAR

1 TSP SALT

⅓ TSP EACH GINGER, CLOVES, ALLSPICE

¼ TSP FRESHLY GRATED NUTMEG

½ TSP GROUND CINNAMON

¾OZ (20G) FRESH YEAST, CRUMBLED

9FL OZ OR 1⅛ CUPS (250ML) MILK AT
    BODY TEMPERATURE

1 LARGE EGG, BEATEN

4OZ OR ABOUT ⅘ CUP (115G) RAISINS

3OZ OR ½ CUP (85G) SULTANAS (WHITE RAISINS)

2OZ (55G) CANDIED LEMON PEEL, FINELY CHOPPED

CROSSES

3½FL OZ OR ⅖ CUP + 1TBSP (100ML) WATER

3½OZ OR ⅘ CUP (100G) ALL-PURPOSE FLOUR

1 MEDIUM EGG

GLAZE

2 TBSP GOLDEN SYRUP (OR 1 TBSP EACH LIGHT
    CORN SYRUP AND HONEY, MIXED)

banana, maple syrup, and pecan rolls

THESE LITTLE ROLLS ARE MY FRIEND BRIDGET'S VARIATION ON BRITISH "TOASTED TEACAKES." THEY ARE GREAT SERVED ON A COFFEE BREAK AND ARE DELICIOUS TOASTED WITH BUTTER AND AN EXTRA DRIZZLE OF MAPLE SYRUP.

18OZ OR 3⅗ CUPS (500G) WHITE BREAD FLOUR

1 TSP FINE SEA SALT

½OZ (15G) FRESH YEAST, CRUMBLED

15FL OZ OR 1⅞ CUPS (425ML) WATER AT BODY TEMPERATURE

2 TBSP MAPLE SYRUP

2 BANANAS, PEELED AND CHOPPED

4OZ OR ABOUT 1 CUP (115G) SHELLED PECANS, TOASTED AND ROUGHLY CHOPPED

1 Sift the flour and salt into a large bowl and make a well in the center. Cream the yeast with 1 tbsp of the water and put into the well in the flour along with most of the maple syrup. Mix, gradually adding enough of the remaining water to make a soft, smooth dough.

2 Tip the dough out onto a lightly floured surface and knead for 10-15 minutes, until it is smooth and elastic. Place in a lightly oiled bowl, cover with a damp dish towel, and leave to rise for 1 hour, or until it has doubled in size.

3 Punch down and knead the dough on a lightly floured surface for 2-3 minutes, then knead or chafe to incorporate the bananas and pecans. Divide the dough into 10 balls and place in a batch, nestling together, on an oiled baking sheet. Leave to proof, covered with a damp dish towel, for 30 minutes, or until they have doubled in size.

4 Preheat the oven to 400°F.

5 Bake the rolls for 20-25 minutes, until they have risen and are golden. While they are still warm, drizzle the tops with the remaining maple syrup. Leave to cool on a wire rack before separating them.

variation

Shape the dough into one loaf, preferably free-form, and bake for about 35-40 minutes.

lavender and honey knots

THESE PRETTY BREAD ROLLS ARE SCRUMPTIOUS SERVED WITH BUTTER AND HONEY. THEY CAN ALSO EASILY BE MADE INTO A LOAF (*SEE* VARIATION BELOW).

1 Preheat the oven to 425°F.

2 Put half the white and whole-wheat flours into a large bowl and make a well in the center. Dissolve the yeast in 150ml (5fl oz or ⅝ cup) of the water and pour into the well in the flour. Mix well for 5 minutes, then leave to rest for 30 minutes, covered with a damp dish towel.

3 Add the remaining flours and water and the salt, honey, and lavender to the dough and knead it well on a lightly floured surface for 5 minutes, until it is smooth and elastic. Leave to rest for 30 minutes in a lightly oiled bowl covered with a damp dish towel until it has doubled in size.

4 Punch down the dough and knead for 2-3 minutes on a lightly floured surface. Divide the dough into 12 equal pieces. Working with one piece at a time, roll the dough backward and forward until it is about 12-16 inches in length. Tie each strip into a loose knot and place on a greased baking sheet. Do the same with all the other pieces of dough. Mix the egg and honey together for the glaze and brush it onto each roll. Cover and leave to proof for 30-40 minutes.

5 Bake for 15-20 minutes, until the knots are risen and golden and the base of the bread sounds hollow when tapped with the fingertips. Leave them to cool on a wire rack.

variation

To make one free-form loaf, mix half of the flours, all the yeast, and half the water and leave to rest for four hours. Add the remaining ingredients, knead, then leave to rest for a further half-hour. Punch down, shape into a ball with a circle scored on the top, and leave to proof for an hour. Bake for 30 minutes.

DOUGH

9OZ OR 1⅘ CUPS (250G) WHITE BREAD FLOUR

9OZ OR 2 CUPS + 2 TSP (250G) WHOLE-WHEAT FLOUR

1OZ (25G) FRESH YEAST, CRUMBLED

10FL OZ OR 1¼ CUPS (300ML) WATER AT BODY TEMPERATURE

1 TBSP FINE SEA SALT

3 TBSP (75ML) HONEY

1 TBSP CULINARY LAVENDER FLOWERS

GLAZE

1 LARGE EGG, BEATEN

1 TBSP HONEY

pizzas and flatbreads

ALL BREADS WOULD HAVE BEEN FLAT AT ONE TIME, BEFORE THE POWER OF LEAVENING WAS DISCOVERED (THROUGH AIRBORNE YEASTS, STILL THE BASIS OF THE MOST TRADITIONAL SOURDOUGH BREADS) AND BEFORE OVENS WERE COMMONLY AVAILABLE. BASIC MIXTURES OF GRAIN AND WATER WOULD HAVE BEEN BAKED ON A FLAT SURFACE: A STONE BESIDE A FIRE OR A GRIDDLE HUNG ABOVE A FIRE. THE OATCAKE ON PAGE 163 IS A CLASSIC EXAMPLE OF AN OLD YEAST-FREE FLATBREAD. MANY INTERNATIONAL BREADS ARE STILL FLAT IN ESSENCE, ALTHOUGH THEY MIGHT NOW USE LEAVENING AGENTS SUCH AS YEAST: THE MIDDLE EASTERN PITA, FOR INSTANCE (*SEE* PAGE 47) AND THE INDIAN *NAAN*.

THE PIZZA STARTED OFF AS A SIMPLE BREAD IN MUCH THE SAME WAY, BEFORE THE CANNY NEAPOLITANS DECIDED TO ADD TOPPINGS. PIZZA IS NOW A WORLDWIDE PHENOMENON, BUT THERE IS NOTHING QUITE LIKE A HOMEMADE ONE. THERE ARE FOUR PIZZA DOUGHS HERE: ONE VERY QUICK TO MAKE, THE OTHERS SLOWER. ALL ARE DELICIOUS, AND THEY

ARE SO VARIABLE: YOU CAN MAKE LARGE, CIRCULAR PIZZAS TO SHARE, PIZZA "SWISS ROLLS," *CALZONI* (FOLDED PIZZAS), OR TINY PIZZA CANAPÉS TO SERVE AT A PARTY.

TO SAVE ON TIME, YOU COULD DO AS I DO: MAKE DOUBLE THE QUANTITY OF DOUGH, AND FREEZE HALF. THERE IS ABSOLUTELY NOTHING WRONG WITH FREEZING DOUGH; IN FACT, ONCE OUT OF THE FREEZER AND DEFROSTING, IT IS RISING AT THE SAME TIME. I TAKE MY DOUGH OUT FIRST THING IN THE MORNING, AND WHEN I COME HOME AT NIGHT IT IS READY TO BAKE—SO, IN ESSENCE, THERE IS NO TIME INVOLVED AT ALL!

KIDS LOVE FLATBREADS AND PIZZAS, SO THIS IS QUITE A CHILD-FRIENDLY CHAPTER. THEY COULD HELP TO MAKE THE DOUGH AS WELL AS CHOOSE THEIR OWN TOPPINGS FOR PIZZAS. EVEN DIET-CONSCIOUS PEOPLE CAN TAKE TO THESE BREADS—THEY ARE "SKINNY," WITH ALL THE TASTE BUT WITH MUCH LESS BREAD.

semolina pizza dough

THIS IS A CLASSIC, TENDER NEAPOLITAN DOUGH, MADE WITH HARD-WHEAT SEMOLINA. IT HAS TAKEN ME A LONG TIME TO PERFECT THIS RECIPE AND THE RESULT IS A MUCH CRISPER CRUST THAN MANY RECIPES YIELD. IF YOU HAVE THE TIME, THIS DOUGH IS EVEN BETTER IF ALLOWED TO RISE FOR FOUR TO SIX HOURS.

1 Combine the flours and salt in a large bowl and make a well in the center. Dissolve the yeast in 2 tbsp of the water. Gradually add the yeast mixture to the well in the dough, along with enough of the remaining water to create a soft, pliable dough.

2 Knead the dough on a lightly floured surface for 10 minutes, until it is smooth and elastic. Shape the dough into a ball, cover with a damp dish towel, and leave it to rise for 1 hour, or until it has doubled in size.

3 Punch down the dough and divide it into two pieces. Roll these into circles and place them on a floured work surface. Cover with a damp dish towel and leave to proof for 30 minutes.

4 Punch down the dough, then roll it out and shape accordingly (*see* individual recipes).

5½OZ OR 1 CUP + 2 TSP (150G) FINE SEMOLINA FLOUR

3½OZ OR ⅘ CUP (100G) ITALIAN "00" FLOUR (OR HALF ALL-PURPOSE AND HALF CAKE FLOUR, THE LATTER NOT SELF-RISING)

1 TSP FINE SEA SALT

¼OZ (10G) FRESH YEAST, CRUMBLED

2FL OZ OR ¼ CUP (50ML) WATER AT BODY TEMPERATURE

quick-rise pizza dough

THE SEMOLINA PIZZA DOUGH IS WONDERFUL, BUT IT TAKES UP TO 6 HOURS TO RISE (ALTHOUGH IT CAN BE DONE IN 1 HOUR; *SEE* PAGE 75). THIS ONE, HOWEVER, TAKES MUCH LESS TIME AND IS STILL VERY GOOD, WITH A CRISP, TASTY RESULT.

9OZ OR 1⅔ CUPS (250G) WHITE BREAD FLOUR

1 TSP FINE SEA SALT

¼OZ (10G) FRESH YEAST, CRUMBLED

2FL OZ OR ¼ CUP (50ML) WATER AT
    BODY TEMPERATURE

1 Mix the flour and salt in a large bowl and make a well in the center. Dissolve the yeast in the water, then add it to the well in the flour and mix well to form a raggy dough.

2 Tip the dough out onto a lightly floured surface and knead it for 10 minutes. Shape it into a ball, place in an oiled bowl, cover with a damp dish towel, and leave to rise for 1 hour.

3 Punch down the dough and knead it on a lightly floured surface for another 10 minutes. Return the dough to the bowl, cover again, and leave to proof for a further hour.

4 Punch down the dough and shape it accordingly (*see* individual recipes).

slow variation

A classic dough for making Neapolitan-style pizza uses exactly the same ingredients as this recipe, but it just needs longer for kneading, rising, and proofing. The taste and texture are infinitely superior.

Knead for a further 10 minutes until the dough is strong, soft as silk, and very elastic. Shape it into a ball and leave it on the lightly floured surface, covered with a clean bowl, for 4 hours, or until it has doubled in size.

Punch down the dough and divide it in half. Cover the pieces again and leave them to proof for 2 hours, or until they have doubled in size.

Punch down and shape accordingly (*see* individual recipes).

red onion and goat cheese pizza tart

THIS IS MY VARIATION OF THE TRADITIONAL FRENCH PIZZA-TYPE TART, *PISSALADIÈRE*. IT IS OFTEN MADE USING PASTRY BUT IS EQUALLY DELICIOUS WITH A BREAD BASE. IT MAKES A GREAT VEGETARIAN LIGHT LUNCH WITH SALAD.

1 Mix the flour and salt into a large bowl and make a well in the center. Cream the yeast with 1 tbsp of the water and add it to the well in the flour with the olive oil and remaining water. Mix until the dough comes away from the sides of the bowl.

2 Tip the dough onto a lightly floured surface and knead for 5 minutes, until it is smooth. Place it in a lightly oiled bowl, cover with a damp dish towel, and leave to rise for 1 hour, or until it has doubled in size.

3 Meanwhile, heat the oil for the topping in a frying pan. Add the onion and fry gently for 15 minutes, until it has softened. Stir in the sugar and garlic. Fry for 5 more minutes, until the onions are beginning to caramelize, then stir in the thyme. Set aside to cool slightly.

4 Punch down the dough, then tip it out onto a lightly floured surface and knead for 5 minutes, until it is smooth and elastic. Roll it out to a circle of about 12 inches in diameter. Spoon the onions evenly over the dough base, leaving a narrow border of dough around the edges. Scatter the goat cheese over it and season with salt and pepper. Cover loosely and leave to proof for 30 minutes.

5 Preheat the oven to 425°F.

6 Bake the tart for 12–15 minutes, until the dough looks golden. Cool a little on a wire rack, and eat hot, warm, or cold.

DOUGH

9OZ OR 1⅘ CUPS (250G) WHITE BREAD FLOUR

½ TSP FINE SEA SALT

½OZ (15G) FRESH YEAST, CRUMBLED

5FL OZ OR ⅝ CUP (150ML) WATER AT BODY TEMPERATURE

2 TBSP OLIVE OIL

TOPPING

3 TBSP OLIVE OIL

3 MEDIUM RED ONIONS, PEELED AND THINLY SLICED

1 TSP SUPERFINE SUGAR

2 GARLIC CLOVES, PEELED AND CRUSHED

1 TBSP ROUGHLY CHOPPED FRESH THYME

5½OZ OR ABOUT ½ CUP (150G) GOAT CHEESE, CRUMBLED

SEA SALT AND FRESHLY GROUND BLACK PEPPER

pizza tartlets

THROUGHOUT ITALY, THERE ARE AS MANY TOPPINGS FOR PIZZA AS THERE ARE SAUCES FOR PASTA. JUST ABOUT
ANY COMBINATION OF INGREDIENTS CAN BE TRANSFORMED INTO A CRISPY, BAKED DELICACY. PIZZA TARTLETS
ARE A COMMON FESTIVE FOOD AMONG SICILIANS.

1 RECIPE QUICK-RISE PIZZA DOUGH (*SEE* PAGE 76),
 OR OTHER OF CHOICE

OLIVE OIL

SEA SALT AND FRESHLY GROUND BLACK PEPPER

TOPPING 1

1 SMALL RED PEPPER

1 SMALL YELLOW PEPPER

7OZ (200G) MIXED MUSHROOMS, I.E. PORCINI
 OR FIELD, FINELY CHOPPED

3½OZ OR 1 SCANT CUP (100G) FONTINA CHEESE,
 SHAVED (USE FRESH MOZZARELLA
 IF UNAVAILABLE)

TOPPING 2

4 SMALL ZUCCHINIS

4 RIPE PLUM TOMATOES, HALVED

1 TSP FINELY CHOPPED FRESH MINT

3½OZ (100G) SMOKED MOZZARELLA OR SCAMORZA
 CHEESE, CUT INTO HALF-INCH CUBES

TOPPING 3

1 SMALL EGGPLANT, PEELED AND CUT INTO
 HALF-INCH CUBES

1 X 3½-4OZ (100G) CAN TUNA IN BRINE, DRAINED

3½OZ (100G) BUFFALO MOZZARELLA, CUT INTO
 HALF-INCH CUBES (USE REGULAR MOZZARELLA
 IF UNAVAILABLE)

12 BLACK OLIVES, STONED AND CHOPPED

TOPPING 4

2 MEDIUM ONIONS, PEELED AND FINELY SLICED

ABOUT 2½FL OZ OR A ¼ CUP + 1 TBSP
 (75ML) WATER

A HANDFUL OF ARUGULA LEAVES, STEMS REMOVED

½ GARLIC CLOVE, PEELED AND CRUSHED

½ TSP PAPRIKA

1 Preheat the oven to 400°F.

2 Roast the peppers for Topping 1 for 20 minutes. Leave to cool, then skin and deseed, and cut into thin strips. Set aside. Keep the oven on, and turn it up to 425°F.

3 Heat about 2 tbsp of the oil in a frying pan over a medium heat and sauté the eggplant for Topping 3 for 7-9 minutes, stirring constantly. Season with salt and pepper and set aside. Heat a little more oil in the same pan and sauté the mushrooms for Topping 1 for 4 minutes. Season with salt and pepper. Set aside.

4 Add a little more oil to the same pan and sauté the onion for Topping 4. Add the water and cook for 8 minutes, or until the onion is coarsely wilted.

5 Parboil the zucchini for Topping 2 in salted water for 5 minutes. Lift out with a slotted spoon, cut into thin slices, and set aside. Parboil the arugula for Topping 4 in the same water for 2 minutes. Drain and squeeze dry.

6 Heat a little more olive oil in the frying pan over a high heat and sauté the tomatoes for Topping 2 for 8 minutes, stirring constantly. Transfer to a bowl, toss with the mint, and set aside.

7 Heat 1 tbsp of oil in a frying pan, add the garlic and arugula for Topping 4, and toss well for 1 minute. Season with salt and pepper, and set aside.

8 Oil 12 x 3-inch round individual tart pans.

9 Put the punched-down dough on a lightly floured surface and knead for 2-3 minutes. Roll into a large rectangle about ⅛-inch thick. Cut into 12 x 3-inch circles and arrange in the tart pans, pressing the edges against the sides. Cover the surface of each tart with baking parchment and weigh it down with baking beans.

10 Bake the tart cases for 10 minutes. Remove from the oven and remove the beans and paper.

11 Top three of the little tarts with peppers, mushrooms, and fontina; three with zucchini, tomato, mint, and mozzarella; three with eggplant, tuna, mozzarella, and olives; and three with onion, arugula, garlic, and paprika.

12 Return to the oven and bake for 10 minutes. Remove from the tart pans and serve immediately.

little pizzas

PIZZETTE ARE THE PERFECT APPETIZER PIZZAS. FOR A CHILDREN'S PARTY, OFFER THEM WITH A VARIETY OF TOPPINGS, SUCH AS ROASTED RED AND YELLOW PEPPERS WITH PINE NUTS, OR A CLASSIC TOMATO SAUCE WITH BASIL AND MOZZARELLA. EXPERIMENT WITH THE TOPPINGS TO CREATE A VARIETY OF GORGEOUS FLAVORS.

DOUGH

1 RECIPE QUICK-RISE PIZZA DOUGH (*SEE* PAGE 76), OR OTHER OF CHOICE

2 TSP FINELY GRATED UNWAXED LEMON ZEST

TOPPING

5½OZ (150G) TOMATOES, CUT INTO 1-INCH CHUNKS

1 RED ONION, PEELED AND THINLY SLICED

3 TBSP OLIVE OIL

1 TBSP CAPERS, RINSED AND DRAINED

1 TBSP FINELY CHOPPED FRESH FLAT-LEAF PARSLEY

1 TBSP EXTRA-VIRGIN OLIVE OIL

1 Preheat the oven to 400°F for at least 30 minutes with a pizza stone inside, if you have one. Otherwise preheat a heavy baking sheet.

2 Make the dough and knead the lemon zest into it as you punch it down. Divide the dough into 12 pieces and form each piece into a ball. Place on a lightly floured work surface, cover with a damp dish towel, and leave to proof for 10 minutes.

3 Punch down the dough, then pat and stretch each ball to a half-inch thickness, leaving the outer edge slightly thicker. Each round will be about 4 inches in diameter.

4 Place each round on a floured double pizza paddle or baking sheet. Lightly brush the rounds with olive oil. Drop the tomato and onion over the tops of the rounds. Drizzle with oil, and slide the pizzas onto the pizza stone or heavy baking sheet.

5 Bake for 4–5 minutes, or until the edges are golden brown. Remove from the oven, and sprinkle with capers, parsley, and the extra-virgin olive oil. Serve immediately.

mini fried potato pizzas

CULLURELLI ARE SMALL FRIED PIZZAS ASSOCIATED WITH THE TRADITIONAL MEATLESS MEALS SERVED ON CHRISTMAS EVE IN ITALY. IN SOVERATO, A SMALL COASTAL VILLAGE ON THE CALABRIAN "INSTEP" OF THE ITALIAN BOOT, THESE DELICIOUS PIZZAS ARE MADE OUTDOORS IN HUGE COMMUNITY FRYING PANS PLACED OVER WOOD-BURNING FIRES.

1 Put the flour and salt in a large bowl, mix, and make a well in the center. Dissolve the yeast in some of the water. Add 1 tbsp of the oil and the potato to the well, along with the dissolved yeast, and mix with enough of the remaining water to make a damp dough.

2 Turn the dough out of the bowl and knead well on a lightly floured work surface for about 10 minutes, until the mixture is smooth and elastic. Return to a clean bowl, cover with a clean dish towel, and leave to rise for 1 hour.

3 Punch down the dough and knead again on a lightly floured surface for 5 minutes. Allow the dough to relax for 5 minutes before pinching off walnut-sized pieces and rolling them into 2-inch rounds. Put the rounds on a lightly floured surface and continue rolling small pieces until all the dough has been used up.

4 Heat 2 inches of olive oil in a heavy frying pan. Fry the pizza rounds three or four at a time until they are golden on both sides. Remove them with a slotted spoon, drain on paper towels, and serve immediately.

10½OZ OR 2 CUPS + 1 TBSP (300G) WHITE BREAD FLOUR

1½ TSP FINE SEA SALT

¼OZ (10G) FRESH YEAST, CRUMBLED

3½FL OZ OR ⅜ CUP + 1 TBSP (100ML) WATER AT BODY TEMPERATURE

OLIVE OIL

1 MEDIUM OLD POTATO, BOILED, PEELED, AND PUT THROUGH A MOULI GRATER OR SIEVE

fried stuffed pizzas

LITTLE FRIED SNACKS LIKE THESE ARE COMMON ON THE STREETS OF NAPLES. THEY MAKE A REALLY SATISFYING LUNCH, AND BECAUSE THEY'RE SEALED, THEY ARE EMINENTLY PORTABLE.

1 In a frying pan, heat the olive oil on medium and sauté the onion until the edges are golden: about 4–5 minutes. Add the spinach and cook for 5 minutes, until wilted. Remove from the heat and cool. Stir in the cheeses, mix well, and season with salt and pepper to taste. Set aside.

2 Knead the punched-down dough on a lightly floured surface for 2–3 minutes. Divide it into 12 pieces. Pat and stretch each piece to about a quarter-inch thickness with a diameter of about 5 inches. Divide the filling evenly among the rounds, leaving a half-inch rim. Fold each round in half, rolling the bottom edge over the top and pinching to seal firmly.

3 In a large frying pan, heat 2 inches of olive oil for frying. Fry the *calzoni* for 2–3 minutes on each side, or until the edges are golden brown. Drain well on paper towels and serve at once.

DOUGH

1 RECIPE QUICK-RISE PIZZA DOUGH (*SEE* PAGE 76), OR OTHER OF CHOICE

OLIVE OIL

FILLING

3 TBSP OLIVE OIL

1 SMALL ONION, PEELED AND DICED

10½OZ (300G) FRESH SPINACH, WASHED, TOUGH STEMS REMOVED

4½OZ OR A GENEROUS ½ CUP (125G) RICOTTA CHEESE

3OZ OR ⅖ CUP (85G) FRESHLY GRATED PARMESAN

2OZ (55G) GORGONZOLA (OR OTHER BLUE) CHEESE, CRUMBLED

SEA SALT AND FRESHLY GROUND PEPPER

sicilian stuffed pizza

SFINCIONE (AS THIS IS KNOWN IN ITALY) IS A POPULAR SICILIAN STUFFED PIZZA. THIS VERSION, WITH ITS SIMPLE AND HEARTY INGREDIENTS, QUALIFIES AS THE ULTIMATE COMFORT FOOD.

DOUGH

1 RECIPE QUICK-RISE PIZZA DOUGH (*SEE* PAGE 76), OR OTHER OF CHOICE

FILLING

1 MEDIUM EGGPLANT, PEELED AND DICED

FINE SEA SALT AND FRESHLY GROUND BLACK PEPPER

OLIVE OIL

1 SMALL ONION, PEELED AND FINELY CHOPPED

5½OZ (150G) GROUND PORK

1 GARLIC CLOVE, PEELED AND FINELY CHOPPED

7 FRESH TOMATOES, DESEEDED AND CHOPPED

1 TBSP TOMATO PASTE

2 PINCHES DRIED OREGANO

1 Spread the eggplant pieces out in one layer on a baking sheet. Sprinkle with salt and cover with another baking sheet. Leave for about 10 minutes. Rinse, drain, and pat the eggplant dice dry with paper towels.

2 Heat 3 tbsp of oil in a medium frying pan over a medium heat and cook the onion until it is softened but not brown: about 2 minutes. Add the pork and cook until it is slightly browned: about 4–5 minutes. Add the eggplant and garlic and cook for a further 4–5 minutes, stirring frequently. Add the tomatoes, tomato paste, oregano, and some salt and pepper and cook until the mixture has thickened: another 20 minutes. Adjust the seasoning to taste and set aside.

3 Preheat the oven to 400°F for at least 30 minutes with a pizza stone inside (if you have one). Otherwise preheat a heavy baking sheet.

4 Knead the punched-down dough on a lightly floured surface for 2–3 minutes, then divide it into six pieces. Pat, then stretch the pieces to a thickness of half an inch and a diameter of about 10 inches. Place three of the rounds on a flour-dusted pizza paddle or a baking sheet. Spread some of the filling in the center of each pizza, leaving a half-inch rim. Top with another round of dough, and pinch the edges to seal. With a sharp knife, make three slashes on the top and brush with olive oil.

5 Slide the three pizzas onto the pizza stone or baking sheet and bake for 20 minutes, or until the edges are golden brown. Remove from the oven, cut in half, and serve at once.

spinach and olive stuffed pizza

THIS PIZZA DOUGH ENCLOSES A FILLING OF SPINACH AND OLIVES, SEASONED WITH GARLIC AND CHILI, LIKE A LARGE PARCEL. IT IS A DELICIOUS LUNCH OR SUPPER MEAL SERVED WITH A SALAD, OR A GREAT PICNIC BREAD. I FIRST ENCOUNTERED THIS RECIPE AT NAPLES AIRPORT, AND IT WAS THE FIRST TIME I HAD SEEN SPINACH IN A BREAD CASING.

1 To prepare the filling, peel and slice the onion and crush the garlic and red chili. Wash the spinach well and chop roughly, discarding any coarse stalks. Heat the oil in a saucepan, add the onion, and cook it for about 5 minutes, until it is soft. Add the garlic and chili and cook for 1 minute. Add the spinach and olives and cook until the spinach just begins to wilt. Remove from the heat and stir in the cheese. Season with salt and pepper.

2 When the dough has risen, punch it down, then turn it onto a lightly floured surface and knead for 2-3 minutes. Divide it in half and roll out each half into a 13-inch round.

3 Place one round on a greased baking tray. Spread the filling over the round. Dampen the edge and place the remaining dough on top. Pinch the edges together to seal. Leave it to proof in a warm place for 20-30 minutes, or until the dough has puffed up.

4 Preheat the oven to 400°F.

5 Brush the dough with extra oil and sprinkle with coarse salt. Bake for about 25 minutes, until it is golden brown. Serve hot, warm, or cold.

DOUGH

1 RECIPE QUICK-RISE PIZZA DOUGH (*SEE* PAGE 76), OR OTHER OF CHOICE, NOT PROOFED

EXTRA-VIRGIN OLIVE OIL

COARSE SEA SALT AND FRESHLY GROUND BLACK PEPPER

FILLING

1 LARGE RED ONION

1 GARLIC CLOVE

HALF A DRIED RED CHILI

1LB 10OZ (750G) FRESH TENDER SPINACH

1 TBSP OLIVE OIL

4OZ (115G) PITTED BLACK OLIVES, CHOPPED

3 TBSP FRESHLY GRATED PARMESAN

eggplant, red pepper, and black olive stuffed pizza

THIS RECIPE COMES FROM CAMPANIA, AND THE FILLING IS A COMBINATION OF SICILIAN *CAPONATA* AND CAMPANIAN *PEPERONATA. PANZEROTTO* IS ANOTHER NAME FOR *CALZONE,* OR STUFFED PIZZA, SO THIS IS KNOWN AS *PANZEROTTO ALLA CAPONATA.* IT IS ASSOCIATED WITH THE FEAST OF ST. GERARD, AS ARE A NUMBER OF BREAD- AND CHEESE-BASED DISHES.

DOUGH

1 RECIPE QUICK-RISE PIZZA DOUGH (*SEE* PAGE 76), OR OTHER OF CHOICE

1 SMALL EGG, BEATEN

2 TBSP HEAVY CREAM

2 TBSP FRESHLY GRATED PARMESAN

FILLING

1 MEDIUM EGGPLANT, PEELED AND CUT INTO 1-INCH CUBES

SEA SALT AND FRESHLY GROUND BLACK PEPPER

1 SMALL RED PEPPER

1 SMALL YELLOW PEPPER

3 TBSP OLIVE OIL

2 MEDIUM RED ONIONS, PEELED AND THINLY SLICED

3 TBSP WATER

1 TSP SUPERFINE SUGAR

1 TBSP CAPERS, DRAINED AND RINSED

2 TBSP PINE NUTS

12 BLACK OLIVES, PITTED AND CHOPPED

1 Preheat the oven to 400°F.

2 Toss the eggplant with salt and place it in a colander to drain for 20 minutes.

3 Roast the peppers for 20 minutes. Cool and skin them, then cut them in half, remove the seeds, and cut the flesh into strips. Keep the oven on.

4 Heat half the oil over a low heat, add the onion, and brown it for 8 minutes, stirring constantly. Add the water, sugar, some salt and pepper, the capers, pine nuts, olives, and pepper strips and toss until they are well blended.

5 Rinse the eggplant and dry it on paper towels. Heat the remaining oil over a medium heat and sauté the cubes for 6–7 minutes, stirring constantly. Season with salt and mix with the onion mixture.

6 Put the punched-down dough on a floured work surface and knead for 2–3 minutes. Roll into a 20-inch circle that is a quarter-inch thick. Place the vegetables on one half of the circle, fold the dough over the filling, and press the edges together to seal them.

7 Mix the egg, cream, and cheese in a bowl, and brush the *calzone* with the mixture to cover all surfaces. Transfer it to a lightly greased baking sheet and bake it for 25 minutes.

8 Remove the bread from the oven, cut it into halves or quarters, and serve immediately.

sardinian pizza

THE PIZZA WAS BORN IN NAPLES, BUT IT HAS TRAVELED ALL OVER MAINLAND ITALY AND THE ISLANDS, AND THIS VERSION IS PARTICULARLY POPULAR IN SARDINIA. THE SALTINESS OF THE ANCHOVIES GOES WONDERFULLY WITH THE NEW SEASON'S TOMATOES—BUT DON'T USE ANY CHEESE BECAUSE YOU DON'T NEED IT WITH FISH. THE PIZZA DOUGH IS RICHER THAN OTHER DOUGHS BECAUSE IT CONTAINS BUTTER AND EGG.

DOUGH

8OZ OR 1⅗ CUPS (225G) WHITE BREAD FLOUR

1 TSP FINE SEA SALT

2¼OZ OR 4 TBSP + 1 TSP (65G) UNSALTED BUTTER, SOFTENED AND DICED

½OZ (15G) FRESH YEAST, CRUMBLED

4 TBSP WATER AT BODY TEMPERATURE

1 LARGE EGG, BEATEN

OLIVE OIL

TOPPING

5 TBSP OLIVE OIL

1LB 10OZ (750G) ONIONS, PEELED AND FINELY SLICED

18OZ (500G) RIPE TOMATOES, SKINNED AND ROUGHLY CHOPPED

FINE SEA SALT AND FRESHLY GROUND BLACK PEPPER

2OZ (55G) ANCHOVY FILETS

A FEW BLACK OLIVES, HALVED AND PITTED

A HANDFUL OF FRESH OREGANO LEAVES

1 To make the dough, mix the flour and salt in a large bowl. Rub in the butter until the texture is like bread crumbs, then make a well in the center. Dissolve the yeast in the water and add it to the well in the flour, along with the egg. Mix to a firm but pliable dough, adding more water if needed.

2 When the dough has come away cleanly from the sides of the bowl, turn it out onto a lightly floured surface and knead it thoroughly for 10 minutes. Gather it into a ball, place in a clean, oiled bowl, and cover with a damp dish towel. Leave to rise until it has doubled in size: about 1½ hours.

3 Meanwhile, make the topping. Heat the olive oil in a heavy pan and fry the onion gently, covered, stirring now and then, until it is soft: about 20 minutes. Add the tomatoes, salt, and pepper and

cook, uncovered, until the sauce is thick: about another 20 minutes. Leave to become cold.

4 When the dough has risen, punch it down and turn it out onto a floured surface. Divide it in two and knead each piece lightly for 2-3 minutes. Pat, then stretch the pieces to a thickness of half an inch and a diameter of about 10 inches. (Or put it into two well-oiled 8-9-inch pizza pans and press out with floured knuckles.) Cover with a damp dish towel and leave to proof for 10 minutes.

5 Preheat the oven to 400°F.

6 Spread the cold topping evenly on the two pizzas. Crisscross them with strips of anchovy and add the olives. Sprinkle with oregano and bake for 25 minutes, until golden brown and bubbling.

tomato, onion, and arugula focaccia

THIS *FOCACCIA*, WITH ITS THUMBPRINT TOP, HAS A MOIST, HERB-SCENTED MIDDLE. MAKE SURE YOU PINCH THE EDGES OF THE DOUGH PROPERLY TO SEAL IN THE FILLING SO THAT IT CANNOT SPILL OUT.

1 Preheat the oven to 400°F. Put the whole tomatoes in a roasting pan (without oil) and roast for 20 minutes.

2 Meanwhile, peel and roughly chop the onions. Heat 1 tbsp of oil in a frying pan, add the onion, and fry for about 5 minutes, until it is softened. Season with salt and pepper. Chop the mozzarella.

3 Punch down the dough, knead it on a lightly floured surface for 2–3 minutes, then divide it in two. Roll out each piece of dough into a thin, 13-inch round. Place one round on an oiled baking sheet.

4 Spread the onions over the round. Add the tomatoes and then the cheese. Sprinkle with arugula and oregano. Dampen the edge and cover with the second round of dough. Pinch the edges together and, using your fingertips, dimple the surface. Cover with a damp dish towel and leave to proof in a warm place for 20 minutes, until it has puffed up a bit.

5 Drizzle the remaining oil over the dough and sprinkle with coarse salt. Transfer it to a hot baking sheet or pizza stone and bake at the same temperature as above for 25 minutes, or until it is golden. Serve warm.

DOUGH

1 RECIPE SIMPLE *FOCACCIA* DOUGH (*SEE* PAGE 36), OR OF CHOICE

FILLING

1LB (450G) CHERRY TOMATOES

2 RED ONIONS

3 TBSP OLIVE OIL

COARSE SEA SALT AND FRESHLY GROUND BLACK PEPPER

6OZ (175G) MOZZARELLA CHEESE

1½ HANDFULS ARUGULA LEAVES

3 TSP FINELY CHOPPED FRESH OREGANO

pizza roll

THIS ROLLED AND SLICED PIZZA IS A DISTINCTLY SOUTHERN ITALIAN DISH. IT CAN BE FILLED WITH YOUR CHOICE OF INGREDIENTS, BUT TYPICALLY IT WOULD HAVE MEAT, GREENS, AND CHEESE INSIDE. IT IS VERY VERSATILE AND CAN BE SERVED AS NIBBLES OR CANAPÉS, AS WELL AS FOR A MEAL.

DOUGH

1 RECIPE QUICK-RISE PIZZA DOUGH (*SEE* PAGE 76), OR OTHER OF CHOICE, JUST KNEADED, DIVIDED INTO TWO CHUNKS

OLIVE OIL

FILLING

3 TBSP OLIVE OIL

HALF AN ONION, PEELED AND FINELY CHOPPED

7OZ (200G) SPINACH LEAVES

4½OZ OR A GENEROUS ½ CUP (125G) RICOTTA CHEESE

SEA SALT AND FRESHLY GROUND BLACK PEPPER

6FL OZ OR ¾CUP (175ML) TOMATO PASSATA

9OZ (250G) BUFFALO MOZZARELLA, IN HALF-INCH-THICK SLICES

1 Put each ball of dough in a separate, lightly oiled bowl. Turn each to coat it with oil. Cover with plastic wrap or a damp cloth and leave to rise in a warm place for 1 hour, until it has doubled in size.

2 Meanwhile, for the filling, heat the olive oil in a frying pan over a medium heat. Add the onion and sauté it until it has softened: about 3-4 minutes. Add the spinach leaves and cook until they are wilted: about another 3 minutes. Remove from the heat, stir in the ricotta, and season with salt and pepper. Set aside to cool a little.

3 Punch down the pieces of dough and knead on a lightly floured surface for 2-3 minutes. Flatten one piece into a rectangle about 12 x 18 inches. Repeat with the second piece of dough. Cover each with a damp dish towel and leave to proof for 10 minutes.

4 Preheat the oven to 400°F and, if you have one, place a pizza stone inside. Otherwise preheat a heavy baking sheet.

5 Pat and stretch each piece of dough to a half-inch thickness, keeping the rectangle shape. Place each piece on a flour-dusted pizza paddle. Spread a thin layer of the passata over each pizza, leaving a half-inch rim. Top with half the spinach and ricotta mixture, then layer on half of the mozzarella.

6 Roll each piece up like a Swiss roll and slide it onto the pizza stone, seam-side down so that it doesn't unroll. Bake for 10-15 minutes, or until the edges are golden brown.

7 Remove from the oven. Cut crosswise into half-inch-thick slices and serve at once.

BIGA: 24 hours   **RISING:** 1½ hours   **PROOFING:** 20 minutes   **BAKING:** 20 minutes   **DRIED YEAST:** ½ tsp (*biga*) and 1 tsp (dough)

MAKES: 1 loaf (to serve about 6)

sage and hazelnut focaccia

SOME OF ITALY'S BEST HAZELNUTS COME FROM PIEDMONT AND THEY TASTE WONDERFUL WITH WILD MOUNTAIN SAGE.
I FIRST ENCOUNTERED THIS *FOCACCIA* IN LIGURIA, A REGION FAMOUS FOR ITS HERBS. THERE, A LITTLE BAKERY MADE
HUGE SHEETS OF IT AND I DISCOVERED THAT THE BAKERS HAD PUT WINE IN THE DOUGH. THIS MAKES THE YEAST
LIGHTER, ALMOST LIKE AN EXTRA FERMENTATION.

1 Put the flour and salt into a large bowl and make a well in the center. Dissolve the fresh yeast in 1 tbsp of the water. Add the yeast liquid, chopped sage leaves, olive oil, and *biga* to the well in the flour and mix. Add the wine and enough of the remaining water to mix to a soft, sticky dough.

2 Turn the dough out onto a floured surface and knead until it is smooth, silky, and elastic: about 10 minutes. Place the dough in a clean, oiled bowl, cover with a damp dish towel, and leave to rise until it has doubled in size: about 1½ hours.

3 Punch down the dough, put it on a lightly floured surface, and chafe, then rest for 10 minutes. Roll it out into approximately a half-inch thickness. Place it on an oiled baking sheet, cover, and leave to proof until it has doubled in size: about 20 minutes.

4 Meanwhile, preheat the oven to 400°F.

5 Press on the top of the dough with your fingers to form dimples. Sprinkle with olive oil, sea salt, fresh sage leaves, and toasted hazelnuts. Bake for 20 minutes, or until it is golden brown and sounds hollow when tapped on the base with the fingertips. Remove from the oven and sprinkle with extra olive oil.

DOUGH

13OZ OR 2⅗ CUPS (375G) WHITE BREAD FLOUR

1½ TSP FINE SEA SALT

¼OZ (10G) FRESH YEAST, CRUMBLED

3FL OZ OR ⅜ CUP (85ML) WATER AT
    BODY TEMPERATURE

20 FRESH SAGE LEAVES, CHOPPED

3 TBSP OLIVE OIL

HALF-RECIPE *BIGA* (*SEE* PAGE 12)

3FL OZ OR ⅜ CUP (85ML) WHITE WINE

TOPPING

OLIVE OIL

COARSE SEA SALT

ABOUT 10 FRESH SAGE LEAVES, TORN

5½OZ (150G) SKINNED HAZELNUTS, TOASTED

olive bread with onion filling

THE ONIONS OF TROPEA, IN CALABRIA, ARE FAMOUS THROUGHOUT ITALY. THEY HAVE A SHORT SEASON, SO IF YOU COME ACROSS THEM, BE SURE TO BUY THEM ON THE SPOT BECAUSE THEY ARE DELICIOUS, AS ARE THE GAETA OLIVES USED HERE. IF YOU CAN RESIST EATING THIS BREAD IMMEDIATELY, IT ALSO TASTES VERY GOOD TOASTED THE NEXT DAY.

DOUGH

18OZ OR 3⅗ CUPS (500G) WHITE BREAD FLOUR

⅛OZ (5G) FINE SEA SALT

½OZ (15G) FRESH YEAST, CRUMBLED

9½FL OZ OR 1 CUP + 1 TBSP (275ML) WATER
    AT BODY TEMPERATURE

2 TBSP OLIVE OIL

2½OZ (75G) GAETA OLIVES, OR THE BEST BLACK
    OLIVES YOU CAN GET, PITTED, SLICED,
    AND DRAINED

FILLING

2 TBSP OLIVE OIL

3 RED ONIONS, PEELED AND CHOPPED

2 BAY LEAVES

1 SPRIG FRESH ROSEMARY, LEAVES PICKED
    FROM THE STALKS

2 TBSP RED-WINE VINEGAR

2OZ (55G) OR ABOUT ⅓ CUP SOFT BROWN SUGAR

TO FINISH

A FEW FRESH ROSEMARY LEAVES

OLIVE OIL

COARSE SEA SALT

1 Sieve the flour and salt onto a work surface and make a well in the center. Dissolve the yeast in the warm water. Add it and the olive oil to the well and slowly incorporate the flour to form a dough.

2 Knead the dough on a lightly floured surface for 10–15 minutes, until it is smooth and elastic. Add the olives and knead or chafe until they are evenly distributed. Put the dough in a lightly oiled bowl, cover with a damp dish towel, and leave for 40 minutes to double in size.

3 Meanwhile, heat the oil for the filling and brown the onions, bay leaves, and rosemary over a low to medium heat, stirring to prevent sticking. Add the vinegar and stir well. Add the sugar and cook over a low heat for 30 minutes. The mixture should be thick, shiny, and a rich red. Allow to cool. (It can be kept in the fridge for two days.)

4 Punch down the dough, then knead it on a lightly floured surface for 2–3 minutes. Divide it in two and shape into balls. Cover and leave to relax for 10 minutes.

5 Roll each ball out into a long, flat, oval shape. Place half the onion mixture and a few extra rosemary leaves slightly off-center on each. Fold each piece over and pinch the edges together. Lightly brush the tops with olive oil and sprinkle with rock salt and rosemary leaves.

6 Place the dough on a lightly greased baking tray, cover with a damp dish towel, and leave to proof for 40 minutes.

7 Preheat the oven to 400°F.

8 Bake the breads for 25 minutes, until they are golden. Brush with olive oil and cool on a wire rack.

spinach, olive, and onion flatbread

THIS IS A *TESTO* BREAD. *TESTO* MEANS "TILE," SO THIS IS A "BREAD OF THE TILE." IT HAILS FROM UMBRIA, WHERE FISHERMEN ON LAKE TRASIMENO, FISHING FOR PIKE, USED TO COOK IT AS A SNACK ON HOT STONES HEATED ON THE FIRE. THERE ARE NUMEROUS TRADITIONAL FILLINGS, BUT THE BREAD DOUGH IS ALWAYS THE SAME.

1 Sift the flour and salt into a large bowl, mix, and make a well in the middle. Mix the yeast with 1 tbsp of water. Pour the yeast liquid, olive oil, and some of the water into the well in the flour. Mix together, gradually adding the rest of the water to form a soft dough.

2 Turn the dough onto a lightly floured work surface and knead vigorously for 10 minutes, until it is smooth. Put it in a clean bowl, cover with a damp dish towel, and leave in a warm place for 45 minutes to double in size.

3 Punch down the dough , and knead for 1-2 minutes. Return it to the bowl, cover, and leave to rise for about another 40 minutes.

4 Meanwhile, for the filling, heat the olive oil in a frying pan. Add the onion, garlic, and chili and cook for about 5 minutes. Add

the spinach and cook for another 5 minutes, until it has wilted. Take it off the heat, add the olives, and season with salt and pepper. Allow to cool. Mix in the mozzarella.

5 Punch down the dough again and knead for 2-3 minutes on a lightly floured surface. Divide it in half and roll out each piece to a 13-inch round. Place one on a lightly oiled baking sheet and spoon the filling on top, leaving a margin around the edge. Dampen the edge, cover with the second round, and pinch the edges together. Cover with a damp dish towel and leave to proof for 30 minutes.

6 Preheat the oven to 400°F.

7 Drizzle the *testo* with olive oil and sprinkle with salt. Bake for 25 minutes, then cool on a wire rack. Serve hot, warm, or cold in wedges.

DOUGH

18OZ OR 3⅗ CUPS (500G) WHITE BREAD FLOUR

2 TSP FINE SEA SALT

½OZ (15G) FRESH YEAST

9FL OZ OR 1⅛ CUPS (250M) WATER AT
    BODY TEMPERATURE

3 TBSP OLIVE OIL

FILLING

2 TBSP OLIVE OIL

1 LARGE RED ONION, PEELED AND SLICED

1 GARLIC CLOVE, PEELED AND CRUSHED

½ DRIED LONG, THIN RED CHILI
    (*PEPERONCINO*), CRUSHED

1LB 10OZ (750G) SPINACH, TRIMMED, WASHED
    AND FINELY CHOPPED

4OZ (115G) PITTED GREEN OLIVES, CHOPPED

SEA SALT AND FRESHLY GROUND BLACK PEPPER

3OZ (85G) MOZZARELLA CHEESE, DICED

FINISH

OLIVE OIL

COARSE SEA SALT

ham and black pepper flatbread

THIS TWELFTH-CENTURY FLATBREAD WITH A FILLED CRUST COMES FROM MY VILLAGE, MINORI IN CAMPANIA, AND THERE ARE MANY RECIPES FOR IT. I THINK YOU WILL ALTER THIS RECIPE AS YOU GROW USED TO IT—IT'S EASILY ADAPTABLE. YOU CAN SERVE IT HOT OR COLD, CUT INTO WEDGES, AND IT'S GREAT FOR PICNICS.

DOUGH

12OZ OR 2⅔ CUPS (350G) WHITE BREAD FLOUR

2 TSP FINE SEA SALT

½OZ (15G) FRESH YEAST, CRUMBLED

9FL OZ OR 1⅛ CUPS (250ML) WATER AT
    BODY TEMPERATURE

2 TBSP MELTED UNSALTED BUTTER

3 TSP FRESHLY GROUND BLACK PEPPER

FILLING

4 LARGE EGGS, HARD-BOILED, PEELED AND DICED

7OZ (200G) PARMA HAM, DICED

6 TBSP MELTED UNSALTED BUTTER

1 Mix the flour and salt into a heap on the work surface and make a well in the center. Dissolve the yeast in 2 tbsp of the water. Add the yeast liquid, butter, 2 tsp of the pepper, and the remaining water to the well. Beat with a fork, incorporating a little flour at a time until a solid ball has formed.

2 Knead on a lightly floured surface for 10–15 minutes, or until the dough is smooth and elastic. Lightly butter a bowl and put the dough in it, cover with a damp dish towel, and leave to rise for 1 hour.

3 Meanwhile, put the diced egg, ham, and 2 tbsp of the melted butter in a bowl and set aside.

4 Preheat the oven to 400°F. Butter a 10-inch round baking pan with 2-inch-high sides (or make the loaf free-form, as opposite).

5 Punch down the dough , then knead for 2–3 minutes. Shape into a large circle. Baste with half the remaining butter and fold the dough in half. Reshape. Create the original circle and dust the surface with the remaining black pepper. Knead for 5 minutes, or until the ingredients are well incorporated, and shape into a 12-inch circle. Arrange in the pan and press the excess dough against the sides, coming up and over them. Cover and leave to proof for 10 minutes.

6 Spoon the egg, ham, and butter mixture around the edges only of the dough casing, then work the overlapping edges over the filling to enclose it and make a rolled crust. The middle will be plain dough.

7 Brush with half the remaining butter and bake for 20 minutes, until golden, basting the top two or three times with more butter.

flatbread with buffalo mozzarella and rosemary

THIS ONE IS A REAL HIT WITH THE LITTLE ONES—PARTICULARLY ANTONIA, MY DAUGHTER. IT'S PERFECT AS AN APPETIZER BEFORE A MEAL, AND IS ALSO A GOOD CHOICE FOR CHILDREN'S PARTIES.

DOUGH

10½OZ OR 2⅓ CUPS (300G) ITALIAN "00" FLOUR (OR USE HALF ALL-PURPOSE AND HAVE CAKE FLOUR, THE LATTER NOT SELF-RISING

1 TSP SALT

¼OZ (10G) FRESH YEAST, CRUMBLED

18FL OZ OR 2¼ CUPS (500ML) WATER AT BODY TEMPERATURE

3 TBSP OLIVE OIL

TOPPING

2 X 3½OZ (100G) BALLS BUFFALO (OR REGULAR) MOZZARELLA, WELL DRAINED AND GRATED

SEA SALT AND FRESHLY GROUND BLACK PEPPER

APPROX. 2 TBSP EXTRA-VIRGIN OLIVE OIL, OR TO TASTE

3 SPRIGS FRESH ROSEMARY, FINELY CHOPPED, OR TO TASTE

1 Put the flour and salt into a large bowl and make a well in the center. Dissolve the yeast in some of the water and add it to the well in the flour, along with the olive oil and the rest of the water. Mix well into a soft dough.

2 Knead the dough on a lightly floured work surface for 10 minutes. The mixture will be soft and pillowy. Place it in a clean, lightly oiled bowl, cover with a damp dish towel, and leave to rise for 1 hour.

3 Punch down the dough and knead for 2–3 minutes on a lightly floured surface. Cover and leave it for a further 10 minutes to rest.

4 Pull out eight balls of the dough with your fingertips, and pat into very thin circles about 12 inches in diameter.

5 Preheat the broiler. Cook the dough circles one by one under the hot broiler for about 2 minutes on each side, until they bubble and brown. Remove them to a chopping board and sprinkle them with mozzarella while they are still hot. Lightly sprinkle with salt and pepper, extra-virgin olive oil, and rosemary.

6 Cut into wedges and devour.

flatbread with grapes

THIS SWEET PIZZA IS TYPICAL OF TUSCANY, WHERE I FIRST ENJOYED IT. SOMETIMES IT HAS FENNEL SEEDS SPRINKLED OVER THE TOP, AND, SERVED WITH A DOLLOP OF MASCARPONE ON THE SIDE, IT IS THE ITALIAN EQUIVALENT OF AN ENGLISH CREAM TEA. IT IS ALSO GOOD AS A SNACK, SERVED WITH A GLASS OF WINE OR EVEN WITH CHEESE.

1 Put the raisins in a bowl, pour in the wine, and leave to soak for at least 2 hours. (You can do this the night before making the bread.)

2 Meanwhile, in a large bowl, mix the flour, salt, and 2oz or a quarter-cup (55g) of the sugar and make a well in the center. Cream the yeast with the warmed milk then add this liquid to the well in the flour. Mix to form a soft dough.

3 Turn the dough onto a lightly floured work surface and knead for 10 minutes, until it is smooth. Put it in a bowl, cover with a damp dish towel, and leave in a warm place for 1 hour, until it has doubled in size.

4 Punch down the dough and knead it again for 1-2 minutes on a lightly floured surface. Drain the raisins.

5 Divide the dough into two even pieces. Roll out each piece to a 8-inch round. Place one round on a floured baking sheet. Cover the round with half the grapes and half the drained raisins. Dampen the edge, cover with the second round, and seal. Top with the remaining grapes and raisins. Cover and leave to proof in a warm place for about 20 minutes, until doubled in size.

6 Preheat the oven to 350°F.

7 Sprinkle the dough with the remaining sugar, then bake for about 45 minutes, or until it is golden. Cool it slightly before serving warm.

DOUGH

12OZ OR 2⅖ CUPS (350G) WHITE BREAD FLOUR

A PINCH OF FINE SEA SALT

3OZ OR ABOUT ⅓ CUP (85G) GOLDEN SUPERFINE SUGAR

¼OZ (10G) FRESH YEAST, CRUMBLED

5FL OZ OR ⅝ CUP (150ML) MILK, GENTLY WARMED

FILLING AND TOPPING

7OZ OR ABOUT 1⅓ CUP (200G) RAISINS

5FL OZ OR ⅝ CUP (150ML) VIN SANTO OR A SWEET DESSERT WINE

18OZ (500G) BLACK GRAPES, DESEEDED

savory breads

MOST OF THE BREADS IN THIS BOOK ARE SAVORY, BUT I THINK OF THE BREADS IN THIS CHAPTER MORE AS "BUSY" BREADS: THEY ARE ESSENTIALLY PLAIN DOUGHS THAT HAVE BEEN ENRICHED WITH A MULTITUDE OF ADDITIONS. IN FACT, BECAUSE THESE BREADS ARE SO ENRICHED ALREADY, MOST WOULD NOT BENEFIT FROM A STARTER SUCH AS A *BIGA*, SO THERE IS NO ADVICE HERE ON MAKING SLOWER VERSIONS OF THE BREADS. BUT WHAT I COULD SAY IS THAT THESE RECIPES SHOULD ACT AS A BASIS UPON WHICH YOU CAN CREATE IDEAS OF YOUR OWN. MY FRIEND BRIDGET'S ROASTED GARLIC AND ZUCCHINI BREAD IS A CASE IN POINT: SHE CAME UP WITH THE IDEA BECAUSE HER SON SO LIKED THE BASIC VEGETABLE DISH. YOU COULD DO THE SAME WITH OTHER VEGETABLES OR COMBINATIONS.

MANY OF THESE RECIPES USE INGREDIENTS THAT ARE UNUSUAL FOR BREADS—INCLUDING BAY LEAVES, GORGONZOLA, CURRY PASTE, MANGO CHUTNEY, AND A NUMBER OF SPICES, TO NAME JUST A FEW—BUT THERE ARE ALSO PLAINER BREADS THAT ARE MADE WITH A LESS USUAL GRAIN, SUCH AS SPELT OR POLENTA.

THESE BREADS ARE SIMPLE TO MAKE, YET MANY OF THEM ARE VERY VISUALLY IMPRESSIVE. THEY ARE ALSO SATISFYING BREADS SUITABLE FOR MANY USES AND OCCASIONS. THEY ARE WONDERFUL IN A CHILD'S PACKED LUNCH, TAKEN ON A PICNIC, OR EATEN AS PARTNERS FOR CHEESE OR SOUP—AND I THINK THEY WOULD BE PERFECT FOR LADIES WHO LUNCH, TO ACCOMPANY A GOOD SALAD...

RISING: 1 hour   **PROOFING:** 30 minutes   **BAKING:** 30-35 minutes   **DRIED YEAST:** 1 tsp   **MAKES:** 1 loaf (to serve 10)

anise and bay crown loaf

THIS RECIPE EVOLVED OUT OF SHEER NECESSITY AND MY LOVE OF ANISE SEEDS AND BAY LEAVES. I THOUGHT THE TWO WOULD MARRY WELL—AND INDEED THEY DO. THE BREAD ALSO LOOKS WONDERFUL. IT IS GOOD SERVED WITH VERY SAVORY FOODS BUT IS EQUALLY DELICIOUS TOASTED FOR BREAKFAST. I'VE SERVED IT WITH CHEESE AT THE END OF A MEAL AND THAT HAS BEEN POPULAR, TOO.

1 Put the anise seeds and water in a small pan and boil for 5 minutes. Pour the mixture into a large bowl and stir in the honey and milk. Let it cool down to body temperature.

2 Sprinkle the yeast over the liquid and stir until completely dissolved. Add the flour 4oz or ⁴⁄₅ cup (115g) at a time, then add the salt. Use only enough flour to make a soft dough.

3 Turn out the dough onto a lightly floured board and knead for 10 minutes, adding flour as necessary to stop it from sticking. The dough should be smooth and tender. Put it in a large bowl and drizzle it with the olive oil. Cover with a damp dish towel and leave to rise for an hour, or until it has doubled in size.

4 When the dough is ready, punch it down, turn it out onto a lightly floured board, and knead for 2 minutes. Flour it lightly, cover it again with the dish towel, and let it rest for 5 minutes.

5 Roll the dough into an 11-inch-long rope. Twist the rope several times and arrange it in a ring on the baking sheet. Pinch the ends together and tuck them under. Make 10 diagonal slashes on the surface and tuck a bay leaf into each slash. Cover the dough and let it proof for 25–30 minutes.

6 Preheat the oven to 400°F. Oil a large baking sheet.

7 Make the egg wash by beating the yolk and water in a small bowl. Brush it over the dough.

8 Bake for 30–35 minutes, or until it is golden and the base sounds hollow when tapped.

DOUGH

1 TSP ANISE SEEDS

9FL OZ OR 1⅛ CUPS (250ML) SPRING WATER

1 TBSP HONEY

9FL OZ OR 1⅛ CUPS (250ML) WHOLE MILK, WARMED

¼OZ (10G) FRESH YEAST, CRUMBLED

18-20 OZ OR 3⅗-4 CUPS (500-550G) WHITE BREAD FLOUR

3 TSP FINE SEA SALT

2 TBSP OLIVE OIL

10 BAY LEAVES

EGG WASH

1 LARGE EGG YOLK

1 TSP WATER

roasted garlic and zucchini bread

MY FRIEND BRIDGET'S SON OLIVER SO LOVED HIS MOTHER'S ZUCCHINIS STIR-FRIED WITH GARLIC THAT SHE TRIED INCORPORATING THEM INTO A BREAD. THE RECIPE WORKED MAGNIFICENTLY AND OLIVER WAS DOUBLY PLEASED!

1 GARLIC BULB

18OZ OR 3⅗ CUPS (500G) WHITE BREAD FLOUR

1½ TSP FINE SEA SALT

½OZ (15G) FRESH YEAST, CRUMBLED

8FL OZ OR 1 CUP (225ML) WATER AT
    BODY TEMPERATURE

2 TBSP OLIVE OIL

4 MEDIUM ZUCCHINIS

COARSE SEA SALT

EXTRA-VIRGIN OLIVE OIL

1 Preheat the oven to 400°F. Put the garlic on a small baking sheet and roast for 15–20 minutes. Leave to cool and switch the oven off.

2 Put the flour and salt in a large bowl and make a well in the center. Cream the yeast with 1 tbsp of the water, then add to the well in the flour with the olive oil and remaining water. Mix until the dough comes away from the sides of the bowl.

3 Tip the dough onto a lightly floured surface and knead for 5 minutes, or until it is smooth and elastic. Leave it to rise in a lightly oiled bowl, covered with a damp dish towel, for 1 hour, or until it has doubled in size.

4 Meanwhile, grate the zucchinis onto a clean dish towel and thoroughly squeeze out all the excess water. Put them in a bowl.

5 Squeeze the roasted garlic out of each clove and mix with the zucchinis. Punch down the dough and knead and chafe the zucchinis and garlic purée into the dough until they are evenly incorporated.

6 Mould the dough into a torpedo shape and turn the ends under. Drizzle lightly with olive oil and sprinkle with coarse sea salt. Cover and leave to proof for a further hour, or until it has doubled in size.

7 Preheat the oven to 400°F.

8 Bake the loaf for 20–30 minutes, until it is golden and the base of the bread sounds hollow when tapped. Drizzle it with extra–virgin olive oil while it is still warm.

rye, dill, and crème fraîche loaf

THIS BREAD IS LOVELY SLICED THINLY, BUTTERED, AND SERVED WITH SMOKED SALMON. IT IS EQUALLY DELICIOUS TOASTED OR SERVED AS *CROSTINI*. SO GO AHEAD: TREAT YOURSELF!

1 Put the flours into a large bowl. Stir in the dill, lemon zest, salt, and sugar and make a well in the center. Dissolve the yeast in 1 tbsp of the water, then pour this into the well in the flour. Mix in along with the crème fraîche and enough of the remaining water to make a smooth dough.

2 Tip the dough onto a lightly floured surface and knead for 5 minutes, or until it is smooth and elastic. Place it in a lightly oiled bowl, cover with a damp dish towel, and leave to rise for 1 hour, or until it has doubled in size.

3 Punch down the dough, then tip it onto a lightly floured surface and knead once more for 5 minutes before shaping it into a round loaf. Place the loaf on a lightly greased baking sheet and make three cuts across the top with a sharp knife. Cover and leave it to proof for 30 minutes.

4 Preheat the oven to 400°F.

5 Bake the bread for 25–30 minutes, until it has browned and the base sounds hollow when tapped with your fingertips. Cool on a wire rack.

6OZ OR 1¾ CUPS (175G) RYE FLOUR

6OZ OR 1½ CUPS (175G) WHOLE-WHEAT FLOUR

4OZ OR ⅘ CUP (115G) WHITE BREAD FLOUR

2 TBSP FINELY CHOPPED FRESH DILL

FINELY GRATED ZEST OF 1 UNWAXED LEMON

2 TSP FINE SEA SALT

1OZ (25G) DARK SOFT BROWN SUGAR

¼OZ (10G) FRESH YEAST, CRUMBLED

9FL OZ OR 1⅛ CUPS (250ML) WATER AT BODY TEMPERATURE

5FL OZ OR ABOUT ½ CUP (150ML) CRÈME FRAÎCHE (USE PLAIN NATURAL YOGURT IF NOT AVAILABLE)

tomato and mozzarella crown loaf

THIS IS A COLORFUL AND DELICIOUS VARIATION ON THE *COURONNE* LOAF DESCRIBED ON PAGE 37. IT IS GREAT FOR
PICNICS OR PARTIES (PERHAPS AS ROLLS; *SEE* VARIATION ON PAGE 110) AND IS SURE TO BE A FAVORITE WITH CHILDREN.

1 RECIPE *COURONNE* DOUGH (*SEE* PAGE 37), RISEN FOR 1 HOUR

4OZ (115G) CHERRY TOMATOES, HALVED

1 X 4OZ (115G) BALL MOZZARELLA, DRAINED AND CHOPPED

A HANDFUL OF FRESH BASIL, TORN

1 Punch down the dough, then knead it on a lightly floured surface for 2–3 minutes. Roll it into a rectangle approximately 10 x 13 inches. Cover the dough with the tomatoes, mozzarella, and basil. Roll it up from the long side until it resembles a Swiss roll. Roll it slightly, then cut lengthwise along the dough, not quite to the end. You will have two long pieces joined at one end; plait them together. Twist into a circle shape, pressing the ends to join.

2 Place the dough on a lightly greased baking sheet. Grease a small bowl and place it in the center of the bread to keep the shape. Leave it to rise, covered with a damp dish towel, for 30 minutes, or until it has doubled in size.

3 Preheat the oven to 425°F.

4 Remove the bowl. Bake the bread for 20–25 minutes, until it is well risen and golden and the base sounds hollow when tapped with your fingertips. Cool it a little on a wire rack, then serve and eat warm (but it's good cold, too).

variation

You could make this mixture into rolls. Divide the dough into 12 balls and bake them for 10–25 minutes. Or the loaf could be made free-form on a greased baking sheet or in an oiled 2lb loaf pan.

braided pepper biscuits

I FIRST ENJOYED THESE HARD BISCUITS IN PUGLIA MANY, MANY YEARS AGO, WITH FAMILY FRIENDS MARIO AND LUISA CARPENTIEI. THE BISCUITS CAN BE EATEN BEFORE LUNCH WITH DRINKS OR JUST AS A *MERENDA* (SNACK) AND ARE DELICIOUS WITH CHUNKS OF PARMESAN CHEESE. THERE ARE SO MANY VARIATIONS ON THIS RECIPE—SOMETIMES THE BISCUITS ARE PLAIN; SOMETIMES THEY ARE FLAVORED WITH FENNEL SEEDS, FOR INSTANCE. ALL ARE GREAT, AND THEY MAKE GOOD GIFTS, TOO. THEY CAN BE MADE UP TO A WEEK IN ADVANCE AND KEPT IN A SEALED CONTAINER.

350G OR 2⅖ CUPS (12OZ) WHITE BREAD FLOUR

2 TSP FINE SEA SALT

3 TSP FRESHLY GROUND BLACK PEPPER

¼OZ (10G) FRESH YEAST

2FL OZ OR ¼ CUP (50ML) WATER AT
    BODY TEMPERATURE

3½OZ OR 7 TBSP (100G) UNSALTED
    BUTTER, MELTED

2 TBSP COARSE POLENTA (OR COARSE CORNMEAL)

1 Heap the flour on a work surface, mix in the salt and pepper, and make a well in the center. Dissolve the yeast in 2 tbsp of the water and pour it into the well in the flour along with the melted butter. Stir with a fork, mixing in a little flour each time and adding more of the remaining water as needed to form a firm dough. Some flour may remain.

2 Knead the dough on a lightly floured surface for 15 minutes, or until it is smooth and soft.

3 Pinch off a walnut-sized piece of dough and roll it into an 8-inch rope. Holding one end in each hand, twist your right hand forward and your left hand backward, as if forming a rolled cord. Seal the two ends together to create a circle and place the dough on a floured

board. Continue until all the dough is used up, spacing the twisted circles well apart. Cover the dough with a damp dish towel and leave it to rise for 1¼ hours, or until it has doubled in size.

4 Preheat the oven to 375°F. Sprinkle two baking sheets with polenta.

5 Transfer the dough circles to the baking sheets, spaced well apart, and bake for 40 minutes. Remove from the oven and cool completely on wire racks before serving.

chestnut and hazelnut spiral bread

THIS BREAD GOES WELL WITH A RICH GAME STEW OR BOEUF BOURGUIGNON. IT IS ALSO GOOD SERVED

AS A FESTIVE BREAD—WITH GOOSE, PERHAPS, AT CHRISTMAS—OR AS ROLLS (*SEE* VARIATION BELOW).

1 Put the flour and salt into a large bowl and make a well in the center. Cream the yeast with 1 tbsp of the water and add it to the flour with the remaining water. Mix until the dough comes away from the sides of the bowl.

2 Tip the dough out onto a lightly floured surface and knead for 5 minutes, until smooth. Place the dough in a lightly oiled bowl, cover with a damp dish towel, and leave to rise for 1 hour, or until it has doubled in size.

3 Punch down the dough, then tip it out onto a lightly floured surface and knead for 5 minutes, until it is smooth and elastic. Place the chestnut purée and hazelnuts on top of the dough and knead and chafe them in until they are evenly distributed. Shape the

dough into a sausage about 12 inches long, tapering at each end. Roll it into a flat coil, place on a greased baking sheet, and leave to proof, covered with a damp dish towel, for 1 hour, or until it has doubled in size.

4 Preheat the oven to 400°F.

5 Dust the loaf with extra flour and bake it for 20-25 minutes, until it is golden and the base of the bread sounds hollow when tapped with your fingertips. Cool it on a wire rack.

variation

This dough can be made into rolls. Divide it into 12 pieces, roll them into balls or make knots, and bake them for 10-12 minutes.

18OZ OR 3⅗ CUPS (500G) WHITE BREAD FLOUR

1 TSP FINE SEA SALT

½OZ (15G) FRESH YEAST, CRUMBLED

9FL OZ OR 1⅛ CUPS (250ML) WATER AT
    BODY TEMPERATURE

1 X 15OZ (425G) CAN SWEET CHESTNUT PURÉE

4OZ (115G) SHELLED HAZELNUTS, TOASTED
    AND ROUGHLY CHOPPED

herb spelt bread

SPELT IS AN ANCIENT ROMAN GRAIN, A FORM OF WHEAT THAT IS ENJOYING A RESURGENCE IN ITALY AND ELSEWHERE. IT IS VALUED AS A GRAIN THAT IS GOOD FOR THOSE WHO ARE GLUTEN- OR WHEAT-INTOLERANT, BUT IT IS WORTHY OF MUCH MORE WIDESPREAD ATTENTION THAN THAT BECAUSE IT IS DELICIOUS, WITH A NUTTY FLAVOR AND GOOD TEXTURE.

1 Put the flour and salt in a large bowl and make a well in the center. Dissolve the yeast in 1 tbsp of the water, then add it to the well in the flour along with the olive oil and enough of the remaining water to make a firm dough.

2 Knead it for 5 minutes on a lightly floured surface, until it is soft to the touch. Leave to rise in a clean, oiled bowl covered with a damp dish towel for 1 hour.

3 Punch down the dough and knead it for 2–3 minutes on a lightly floured surface. Chop the herbs finely, place them on top of the dough, then knead or chafe them into the dough (opposite) until they are well blended. Shape the dough into a loaf and place it in an oiled 1lb loaf pan. Leave to proof, covered with a damp dish towel, for 1 hour, or until it has doubled in size.

4 Preheat the oven to 425°F.

5 Bake the loaf for 25–30 minutes, or until it is golden and the base sounds hollow when tapped with your fingertips. Cool it on a wire rack.

variation

You can vary the herbs used: the herbs here are rather summery, but you could use sage, rosemary, and parsley for a winter loaf, for instance.

18OZ OR 3⅗ CUPS (500G) SPELT FLOUR

1 TBSP FINE SEA SALT

¾OZ (20G) FRESH YEAST, CRUMBLED

14FL OZ OR 1¾ CUPS (400ML) WATER AT BODY TEMPERATURE

2 TBSP OLIVE OIL

1 SMALL BUNCH FRESH BASIL

1 SMALL BUNCH FRESH FLAT-LEAF PARSLEY

1 SMALL BUNCH FRESH MINT

curry bread

THE IDEA FOR THIS BREAD WAS GIVEN TO MY FRIEND BRIDGET BY A FRIEND OF HERS WHO LOVES CURRY BUT IS NOT A FAN OF *NAAN* BREADS. IF YOU PREFER *NAAN*, YOU CAN MAKE THE DOUGH INTO FLATBREADS (SEE VARIATION BELOW).

10FL OZ OR 1¼ CUPS (300ML) MILK

1 TBSP UNSALTED BUTTER

1OZ (25G) FRESH YEAST, CRUMBLED

1LB OR 3⅓ CUPS (450G) WHITE BREAD FLOUR

1 TSP FINE SEA SALT

1 TSP CUMIN SEEDS

1 TBSP MEDIUM CURRY PASTE

1 TBSP FRESH CILANTRO LEAVES, CHOPPED

1 TBSP MANGO CHUTNEY

1 LARGE EGG, BEATEN

MILK AND CUMIN SEEDS, FOR GLAZING

1 Heat the milk and butter together, then allow the mix to cool until it is tepid. Dissolve the yeast in a little of it.

2 Sift the flour and salt into a large bowl. Stir in the cumin seeds and make a well in the center. Stir in the yeast liquid, curry paste, cilantro, chutney, and egg, then pour in the remaining warmed milk-and-butter mixture and mix to a smooth dough.

3 Tip the dough out onto a lightly floured work surface and knead it for 10 minutes, until it is smooth and elastic. Leave it to rise in a lightly oiled bowl covered with a damp dish towel until it has doubled in size: about 1 hour.

4 Punch down the dough, then knead it on a lightly floured surface for a further 5 minutes. Shape it into a torpedo. Slash it down the middle of the loaf with a sharp knife about three times,

then brush it with milk and sprinkle with cumin seeds. Cover and leave to proof for 30 minutes on a lightly greased baking sheet until it is well risen.

5 Preheat the oven to 400°F.

6 Bake the loaf for 30 minutes, until it is golden and sounds hollow when tapped on the base with your fingertips. Leave it to cool a little on a wire rack, then eat while it is still warm.

variation

You could make *naan*-like flatbreads from this mixture to go with curry. Divide the dough into 12, then roll out to thin discs about 5 inches long. Bake them for 12–15 minutes.

bacon, egg, and cheese bread

MY FRIEND BRIDGET FIRST MADE THIS BREAD WITH A COLLEAGUE AT LEITHS SCHOOL OF FOOD AND WINE IN LONDON, WHEN SHE WAS TRAINING. IT HAS SINCE BECOME A FIRM FAVORITE IN HER HOUSEHOLD AND IS REALLY A MEAL IN ITSELF.

1 Sift the flour and salt into a large bowl and make a well in the center. Dissolve the yeast in a little of the water, then stir this yeasty liquid into the flour with enough of the remaining water to make a soft dough.

2 Knead the dough for 10–15 minutes on a lightly floured surface, until it is smooth and elastic. Place it in a lightly oiled bowl, cover with a damp dish towel, and leave to rise for 1 hour.

3 Punch down the dough, then tip it onto a lightly floured surface and knead for 2–3 minutes. Roll it to a rectangle roughly 10 x 13 inches in size. Cover the dough with the remaining ingredients, season with salt and pepper, and roll it into a sausage shape from the long side. Place the seam underneath, and then tuck in each end. Place the loaf on a lightly greased baking sheet, cover with a damp dish towel, and leave to proof for 30 minutes, until it has doubled in size.

4 Preheat the oven to 400°F.

5 Bake the loaf for 25–30 minutes, then leave it to cool on a wire rack.

variation

This mixture can be made into rolls. Divide the dough into 12 equal pieces and wrap them around the filling. Bake them for 12 minutes.

18OZ OR 3⅗ CUPS (500G) WHITE BREAD FLOUR

1½ TSP FINE SEA SALT

1OZ (25G) FRESH YEAST, CRUMBLED

18FL OZ OR 2¼ CUPS (500ML) WATER AT BODY TEMPERATURE

4OZ (115G) BACON, BROILED AND CHOPPED

4 LARGE HARD-BOILED EGGS, SHELLED, AND CHOPPED

4OZ OR ABOUT 1 CUP (115G) GRUYÈRE CHEESE, FRESHLY GRATED

SEA SALT AND FRESHLY GROUND BLACK PEPPER

ricotta bread

THIS BREAD IS GOOD WITH CHEESE. IN THIS VERSION OF THE RECIPE, IT IS FLAVORED WITH FENNEL SEEDS, BUT YOU COULD USE CRISPY BITS OF PANCETTA, WALNUTS, RAISINS, OR FIGS INSTEAD.

DOUGH

½OZ (15G) FRESH YEAST, CRUMBLED

8FL OZ OR 1 CUP (225ML) WATER AT
    BODY TEMPERATURE

4½OZ OR ½ CUP (125G) TUB RICOTTA, AT
    ROOM TEMPERATURE

2 TSP FINE SEA SALT

A PINCH OF FENNEL SEEDS

18OZ OR 3⅗ CUPS (500G) WHITE BREAD FLOUR

2-3 TBSP OLIVE OIL

EGG WASH

1 LARGE EGG YOLK

1 TSP WATER

1 To make the dough, dissolve the yeast in some of the water in a large bowl. Stir in the ricotta, salt, and fennel seeds. Add the flour little by little, using only enough to make a soft dough.

2 Turn the dough out onto a lightly floured work surface. Knead it for 10 minutes, incorporating more flour if necessary to keep the dough from sticking. The dough should be smooth and tender. Transfer it to a large bowl and drizzle and rub olive oil over it. Cover the bowl with a damp dish towel and leave it for 1 hour, or until doubled in size.

3 When the dough is ready, punch it down, turn it out onto a lightly floured work surface, and knead for 2 minutes. Flour the dough lightly and wrap and rest for 5 minutes.

4 Preheat the oven to 400°F. Oil a large baking sheet.

5 Flatten the dough with a rolling pin and shape it into a 13 x 8-inch oval. Transfer the dough to the baking sheet. Cut a 7-inch-long slit lengthwise through the center of the dough, completely through to the baking sheet. Spread the split open slightly. Cover the dough with a damp dish towel and let it proof for 15 minutes.

6 Make the egg wash by beating the egg yolk and water in a small bowl. Brush the egg wash over the surface of the dough. Bake the loaf on the center shelf of the oven for 25–30 minutes, or until it is a rich brown and cooked through. Tap the bottom of the bread with your fingertips—it will sound hollow if it is done. Cool it on a wire rack.

onion and mozzarella bread

THROUGHOUT ITALY, *PALIOS*—HISTORICAL CONTESTS BETWEEN RIVAL TOWNS—ARE FOUGHT BETWEEN RIDERS ON HORSES, RIDERS ON DONKEYS, AND EVEN RIDERLESS PIGS. BUT IN GESSATE, IN LOMBARDY, THE *PALIO DEL PANE* IS FOUGHT BETWEEN PEOPLE ARMED WITH BUCKETS OF WATER, SALT, FLOUR, AND YEAST: ALL THE INGREDIENTS NECESSARY TO BAKE BREAD. THE SUBSEQUENT PEACE IS EXPRESSED IN VARIOUS TYPES OF BREAD THAT ARE MADE AND OFFERED TO THE SPECTATORS—AMONG THEM, THIS WONDERFULLY LIGHT RING TOPPED WITH SAUTÉED ONIONS AND FRESH MOZZARELLA.

1 RECIPE QUICK-RISE PIZZA DOUGH (*SEE* PAGE 76), OR OTHER OF CHOICE

3 TBSP OLIVE OIL

3½OZ OR 7 TBSP (100G) UNSALTED BUTTER

3 LARGE RED ONIONS, PEELED AND THINLY SLICED

FINE SEA SALT

½ TSP SUPERFINE SUGAR

1 TBSP COARSE POLENTA (OR COARSE CORNMEAL)

9OZ (250G) FRESH MOZZARELLA, CUT INTO STRIPS

1 Put the risen pizza dough on a floured work surface and make a large hole in the center without breaking through the underside. Pour in the oil. Knead it for 5 minutes or until the oil is completely incorporated. Transfer it to an oiled bowl, cover with a damp dish towel, and leave to rise for a further half-hour.

2 Heat the butter in a frying pan over a low heat and sauté the onion for 8 minutes, stirring frequently. Season with a pinch of salt and the sugar.

3 Sprinkle a 10 x 12-inch baking sheet with the polenta. Punch down the dough and knead it on a lightly floured surface for 2–3 minutes. Form it into a long, thick sausage shape. Roll into a ring and press the ends together to seal

them. Transfer it to the baking sheet and coat with polenta. Cover with the dish towel and leave to proof for 30 minutes.

4 Preheat the oven to 400°F.

5 Make a large hollow on the surface of the dough circle and fill it with the sautéed onions. Top with the strips of mozzarella and bake it for 25 minutes.

6 Remove the bread from the oven, cool it on a wire rack, and serve it hot or cold, cut into thick slices.

variation

You could make rolls with this mixture. Enclose the filling in small balls of dough and bake them for 10–12 minutes.

potato and gorgonzola focaccia

ON A BOOK-SIGNING AND PUBLICITY TOUR OF THE USA, I MET DIANE, THE MOTHER OF A FRIEND IN CHICAGO (MOTHER AND DAUGHTER ARE FINE COOKS). I WAS DOING A COOKERY DEMONSTRATION, AND AT THE END OF THE EVENING, DIANE PRESSED THIS RECIPE INTO MY HAND AND URGED ME TO TRY IT. I DID—AND IT'S WONDERFUL. I THANK HER VERY MUCH.

1 In a covered saucepan, boil the potatoes for 10-15 minutes, or until they are tender. Drain and mash them, then cool slightly.

2 In a large bowl, mix two-thirds of the flour with the salt. Dissolve the yeast in 2 tbsp of the water and add it to a well in the center of the flour with the olive oil. Mix for a few minutes, then stir in the potatoes and as much of the remaining flour as you can.

3 On a lightly floured surface, knead in enough of the remaining flour to make a stiff dough that is smooth and elastic. This will take about 8-10 minutes. Shape the dough into a ball and place it in an oiled bowl, turning it once to grease the surface. Cover it with a damp dish towel and leave it to rise in a warm place until it has doubled in size: roughly 1 hour.

4 Punch down the dough, cover, and let it rest for 10 minutes.

5 Grease a 15 x 10 x 1-inch baking sheet. Press the dough into the pan; if it is sticky, sprinkle the surface with about 1 tbsp of extra flour. Using your fingertips, make small indentations in the dough. Cover and leave it to proof until it has nearly doubled in size: 30 minutes.

6 Meanwhile, preheat the oven to 375°F.

7 For the topping, mix the tomatoes, oregano, basil, garlic, and pepper and spoon evenly over the dough. Place the artichoke hearts over the tomato-sauce mixture. Cover with the Gorgonzola and shredded mozzarella.

8 Bake for 35 minutes. Serve hot.

DOUGH

2 MEDIUM POTATOES, PEELED AND CHOPPED

18-20 OZ OR 3⅗-4 CUPS (500-550G) WHITE BREAD FLOUR

2 TSP FINE SEA SALT

½OZ (15G) FRESH YEAST, CRUMBLED

9FL OZ OR 1⅛ CUPS (250ML) WATER AT BODY TEMPERATURE

2 TBSP OLIVE OIL

TOPPING

1 X 14OZ (400G) CAN CHOPPED ITALIAN TOMATOES, DRAINED

1 TBSP CHOPPED FRESH OREGANO

2 TBSP TORN FRESH BASIL

1 GARLIC CLOVE, PEELED AND FINELY CHOPPED

½ TSP FRESHLY GROUND BLACK PEPPER

13OZ (375G) QUARTERED ARTICHOKE HEARTS MARINATED IN OLIVE OIL

9OZ (250G) GORGONZOLA (OR OTHER BLUE) CHEESE, CRUMBLED

5½OZ OR 1⅓ CUP (150G) MOZZARELLA, SHREDDED

sweet breads

I HAVE A SWEET TOOTH, SO THIS IS AN IMPORTANT CHAPTER FOR ME. MANY OF THE BREADS HERE ARE NOT ACTUALLY "SWEET," IN TERMS OF HAVING A HIGH SUGAR CONTENT, BUT BECAUSE THEY ARE PACKED FULL OF DRIED FRUIT THEY ARE QUITE SWEET IN FLAVOR. A NUMBER OF THESE BREADS ARE ACTUALLY FOR EATING IN A SAVORY CONTEXT—WITH CHEESE OR DIPS (THE WALNUT BREAD, FOR INSTANCE).

THERE ARE IDEAS HERE FROM VARIOUS COUNTRIES, INCLUDING ITALY, THE USA, FRANCE, ENGLAND, AND SCOTLAND. I HAVE TO SAY THAT THE PRUNE AND CHOCOLATE BREAD ON PAGE 134 IS A REAL ALL-TIME FAVORITE OF MINE—OOZING, GOOEY, DELICIOUS—AND I LIKE TO THINK OF IT AS THE PERFECT PICK-ME-UP FOOD WITH A LITTLE LESS GUILT, BECAUSE

PRUNES ARE SO GOOD FOR YOU. THE OTHERS ARE LESS EXOTIC, BUT THEY ARE ALL GREAT BREADS, GOOD FOR EVERYDAY MEALS, FOR SPECIAL OCCASIONS, AND ESPECIALLY FOR BREAKFAST AND SNACKS.

HOMEMADE BREADS, PARTICULARLY THE MORE UNUSUAL ONES, MAKE VERY GOOD GIFTS. THERE IS NOTHING QUITE LIKE A PRESENT THAT SOMEONE HAS SPENT TIME AND EFFORT ON. MY NEIGHBOR ANN RECENTLY GAVE ME SOME DELICIOUS BREAD, AND I THOUGHT IT SUCH A NICE, NEIGHBORLY THING TO DO. AND ONE OF MY STUDENTS GAVE ME A SEMOLINA LOAF HE HAD BAKED FROM ONE OF MY BOOKS. I WAS VERY TOUCHED; GIVING AND SHARING FOOD IS VERY SPECIAL.

molasses and date bread

THIS IS ONE OF MY FRIEND BRIDGET'S FAVORITE BREADS AND WAS POPULAR WITH HER FRIENDS AND NEIGHBORS WHEN SHE TESTED IT. MOST OF THEM AGREED THAT IT WAS LOVELY SERVED WITH BLUE CHEESE. SLICED AND SPREAD GENEROUSLY WITH BUTTER, IT IS WONDERFUL SERVED WITH A CUP OF TEA AT THE END OF A BUSY DAY.

1 Sift the flours and salt into a large bowl. Some grains from the whole-wheat flour will be caught in the sifter or sieve; tip them into the bowl. Rub in the butter, and make a well in the center. Dissolve the yeast in 2 tbsp of the water, then pour it into the well in the flour, along with the molasses and enough of the remaining water to form a soft, smooth dough.

2 Tip the dough out onto a lightly floured surface and knead it for 10-15 minutes, or until it is smooth and elastic. Leave the dough to rise in a lightly oiled bowl covered with a damp dish towel for 1 hour, or until it has doubled in size.

3 Punch down the dough, then knead it on a lightly floured surface for 2-3 minutes. Press the dates into the top of the dough

and knead or chafe them in until they are evenly distributed. Shape the dough into a round and place it on a lightly greased baking sheet. Dust it heavily with extra white flour and score diagonal lines across the top to make diamond shapes. Cover with a damp dish towel and leave it to proof for 30 minutes, or until it has doubled in size.

4 Preheat the oven to 425°F.

5 Bake for 30-35 minutes, until it is golden and sounds hollow when tapped on the base with your fingertips. Cool on a wire rack.

8OZ OR 1⅘ CUPS (225G) WHITE BREAD FLOUR

8OZ OR 2 CUPS (225G) WHOLE-WHEAT FLOUR

1 TBSP FINE SEA SALT

2OZ OR 4 TBSP (55G) UNSALTED BUTTER, SOFTENED AND DICED

1OZ (25G) FRESH YEAST, CRUMBLED

10FL OZ OR 1¼ CUPS (300ML) WATER AT BODY TEMPERATURE

1 TBSP MOLASSES

3OZ (85G) DRIED DATES, CHOPPED

beer and honey bread

THIS BREAD HAS A WONDERFUL FERMENTED SMELL AND FLAVOR. IT TASTES PARTICULARLY GREAT WHEN SLICED THINLY AND SERVED WITH SOFT GOAT CHEESE, FRESH FIGS, AND A DRIZZLE OF HONEY.

2OZ OR 4 TBSP (55G) UNSALTED BUTTER, SOFTENED

10FL OZ OR 1¼ CUPS (300ML) BROWN ALE
   (OR OTHER DARK BEER)

1 TBSP HONEY

8OZ OR 2 CUPS (225G) WHOLE-WHEAT FLOUR

8OZ OR 1⅗ CUPS (225G) WHITE BREAD FLOUR

1 TSP FINE SEA SALT

1OZ (25G) FRESH YEAST, CRUMBLED

1 LARGE EGG, BEATEN

1 Preheat the oven to 400°F. Lightly butter a 2¼lb loaf pan.

2 In a saucepan, bring the ale, honey, and butter to boiling point, then leave the mixture to cool to body temperature.

3 Sift the flours and salt into a large mixing bowl. Some grains from the whole-wheat flour will be caught in the sifter or sieve; tip them into the bowl and make a well in the center. Dissolve the yeast in 1 tbsp of the beer liquid and pour it into the well in the flour along with the beaten egg and the remainder of the beer liquid. Mix to a soft dough.

4 Knead the dough on a lightly floured surface for 10 minutes, until it is smooth and elastic. Put it into a lightly oiled bowl, cover with a damp dish towel, and leave

to rise in a warm place for 1 hour, or until it has doubled in size.

5 Punch down the dough, then tip it onto a lightly floured work surface and knead for 5 minutes. Shape it into a loaf and place in the prepared pan. Leave to proof, covered with a damp dish towel, for 30 minutes

6 Bake the loaf for 30–35 minutes, until it is golden and sounds hollow when tapped on the base with your fingertips. Cool it on a wire rack.

toffee and banana-filled doughnuts

THIS IS A STRAIGHTFORWARD RAINY-DAY RECIPE TO GIVE THE CHILDREN A FUN AND MEMORABLE TIME. THEY WILL ENJOY FILLING EACH DOUGHNUT WITH TOFFEE SAUCE AND WILL MAKE THEMSELVES SOME DELICIOUSLY STICKY TREATS.

1 Sift the flour into a large bowl. Rub in the butter, then stir in 2⅔ tbsp of the sugar and make a well in the center. Dissolve the yeast in 2 tbsp of the water and pour it into the well along with enough of the remaining water to make a smooth dough.

2 Tip the dough out onto a lightly floured work surface and knead it for 10-15 minutes, until it is smooth and elastic. Leave for 1 hour in a lightly oiled bowl covered with a damp dish towel until it has doubled in size.

3 Punch down the dough and knead it for 2–3 minutes on a lightly floured surface. Split it into 3oz (85g) pieces. Push 2 slices of banana into each piece and shape them into balls. Cover and leave to proof on a floured work surface for 30 minutes.

4 Heat the oil to 325°F in a large, heavy pan. Fry the dough balls in batches for 5-10 minutes, until they are golden. Drain well on paper towels.

5 Put the toffee sauce into a piping bag with a small nozzle. Pipe a little of toffee sauce into each doughnut, then dust them heavily with the remaining superfine sugar. Cool them on a wire rack.

9OZ OR 1⅘ CUPS (250G) WHITE BREAD FLOUR

1OZ (25G) UNSALTED BUTTER, SOFTENED AND DICED

5½OZ OR ¾ CUP (150G) SUPERFINE SUGAR

1OZ (25G) FRESH YEAST, CRUMBLED

5FL OZ OR ⅝ CUP (150ML) WATER AT BODY TEMPERATURE

2 BANANAS, PEELED AND SLICED

SUNFLOWER OIL, FOR DEEP FRYING

1 JAR TOFFEE SAUCE (USE CARAMEL SAUCE IF YOU PREFER)

lemon loaf

THIS BREAD IS LOVELY TOASTED WITH BUTTER AS A BREAKFAST BREAD, AND MY FRIEND BRIDGET'S DAUGHTER LOVES IT MADE INTO HONEY SANDWICHES FOR HER SCHOOL LUNCH BOX.

14OZ OR 2⅗ CUPS (400G) WHITE BREAD FLOUR

3½OZ OR 1 CUP (100G) RYE FLOUR

1 TBSP FINE SEA SALT

2½OZ OR 5 TBSP (70G) UNSALTED BUTTER, SOFTENED AND DICED

2½OZ OR ABOUT ⅓ CUP (70G) SUPERFINE SUGAR

1OZ (25G) FRESH YEAST, CRUMBLED

10FL OZ OR 1¼ CUPS (300ML) WATER AT BODY TEMPERATURE

2 TBSP OLIVE OIL

FINELY GRATED ZEST OF 5 UNWAXED LEMONS

4OZ (115G) CANDIED LEMON PEEL, FINELY CHOPPED

1 Put the flours, salt, butter, and sugar into a large bowl. Rub in the butter until the mixture is like bread crumbs, then make a well in the center. Cream the yeast with 1 tbsp of the water and add it to the flour along with the olive oil and remaining water. Mix until the dough comes away from the sides of the bowl.

2 Tip the dough out onto a lightly floured surface and knead for 5 minutes until it is smooth. Place it in a lightly oiled bowl, cover with a damp dish towel, and leave to rise for 1 hour, or until it has doubled in size.

3 Punch down the dough, then knead it for 2-3 minutes on a lightly floured surface before kneading or chafing in the lemon zest and candied peel. Shape the dough into two round loaves and place them on a greased baking sheet. Make three cuts across each loaf, cover with a damp dish towel, and leave to proof for 1 hour, until they have doubled in size.

4 Preheat the oven to 400°F.

5 Bake the loaves for 25-30 minutes, until they are golden brown and their bases sound hollow when tapped with your fingertips. Cool them on a wire rack.

lardy cake

THIS RECIPE WAS GIVEN TO MY FRIEND BRIDGET BY A NEIGHBOR WHO ASSURES HER OF ITS AUTHENTICITY. BRIDGET WANTED TO USE BUTTER INSTEAD OF LARD—BUT THEN, OF COURSE, IT WOULDN'T BE A "LARDY CAKE." THIS VERSION OF THE RECIPE HAS FRUIT IN IT, ALTHOUGH SOME PEOPLE OMIT IT.

DOUGH

1LB OR 3⅓ CUPS (450G) WHITE BREAD FLOUR

1 TSP FINE SEA SALT

½OZ (15G) LARD, SOFTENED AND DICED

2 TBSP SUPERFINE SUGAR

1OZ (25G) FRESH YEAST, CRUMBLED

10FL OZ OR 1¼ CUPS (300ML) WATER AT
   BODY TEMPERATURE

FILLING

3OZ OR ABOUT ⅔ CUP (85G) LARD, DICED

3OZ OR ½ CUP (85G) SOFT LIGHT BROWN SUGAR

4OZ OR ABOUT ⅘ CUP (115G) EACH RAISINS AND
   WHITE RAISINS

1OZ (25G) CANDIED LEMON PEEL, CHOPPED

1 TSP MIXED SPICE*

GLAZE

2 TSP SUNFLOWER OIL

2 TBSP SUPERFINE SUGAR

*MIXED SPICE IS A BLEND OF SPICES UNIQUE TO
   THE UK. TO MAKE ONE VERSION, MIX TOGETHER
   THE FOLLOWING: 4 TBSP CINNAMON, 1 TSP
   GINGER, 1 TSP CLOVES, 1 TSP NUTMEG,
   1 TSP ALLSPICE.

1 Sift the flour and salt into a large bowl and rub in the lard. Stir in the sugar and make a well in the center. Dissolve the yeast in 2 tbsp of the water, pour it into the well, and add the remaining water gradually, mixing until you have a smooth dough.

2 Turn the dough out onto a lightly floured surface and knead it for 10 minutes, until it is smooth and elastic. Place it in a lightly oiled bowl, cover with a damp dish towel, and leave to rise for 1 hour.

3 Punch down the dough, then turn it out onto a lightly floured surface and knead for 2-3 minutes. Roll it into a rectangle. Using half the lard for the filling, cover the top two-thirds of the dough with dots of lard. Sprinkle over half the sugar, half the dried fruits and peel, and half the mixed spice. Fold the bottom third up and the top third down, pressing the edges together with a rolling pin. Turn the dough sideways. Roll lightly and cover with the remaining ingredients. Fold as before, then roll. Grease a 10 x 8-inch Swiss-roll pan. Place the dough in the pan, cover it with a damp dish towel, and leave it to proof for 30-40 minutes.

4 Preheat the oven to 400°F.

5 Brush the top with the oil and sprinkle with the sugar. Using a sharp knife, mark a diamond pattern over the top. Bake for 30-40 minutes. Leave the cake to cool in the pan, then cut it into squares to serve.

selkirk bannock

THIS RICH, YEASTED CAKE-BREAD FROM THE SCOTTISH BORDERS IS STUFFED WITH DRIED FRUIT AND IS SAID TO HAVE
EVOLVED AS A WAY OF USING UP LEFTOVER BREAD DOUGH. SOME SAY IT IS THE SCOTTISH EQUIVALENT OF LARDY CAKE.

1 Mix together a little milk and 2 tsp of sugar for the glaze. Set aside.

2 Put the flour and salt in a bowl and make a well in the center. Dissolve the yeast and 1 tsp of sugar in a little of the milk and leave to froth. Melt the butter and lard with the rest of the milk and keep the liquid warm.

3 Mix the yeast liquid with the flour, then add the milk-and-butter mixture, and mix until it forms a soft dough. Knead for a few minutes on a lightly floured surface, then cover with a damp dish towel, and leave until it has doubled in size: about 1 hour.

4 Punch down the dough, then knead it on a lightly floured surface for 2–3 minutes before kneading or chafing in the rest of the sugar and the sultanas. Shape it into two rounds. Put onto an oiled baking sheet, cover again, and leave to proof in a warm place, until it has doubled in size: about 45 minutes.

5 Preheat the oven to 425°F.

6 Bake for 10 minutes, then reduce the heat to 375°F for half an hour. After about 15 minutes, glaze the bannock with the reserved milk-and-sugar glaze.

14FL OZ OR 1¾ CUPS (400ML) MILK AT
    BODY TEMPERATURE

6OZ OR ABOUT ¾ CUP (175G) SUPERFINE SUGAR

2¼LB OR 7⅓ CUPS (1KG) WHITE BREAD FLOUR

A PINCH OF FINE SEA SALT

1OZ (25G) FRESH YEAST, CRUMBLED

4OZ OR ABOUT ½ CUP (115G) UNSALTED BUTTER

4OZ OR ABOUT ½ CUP (115G) LARD

1LB (450G) SULTANAS (WHITE RAISINS)

RISING: 45 minutes   **BAKING:** 10-12 minutes   **DRIED YEAST:** 3½ tsp   **MAKES:** 12 breadsticks

saffron and raisin breadsticks

SAFFRON IS PROBABLY THE MOST EXPENSIVE SPICE IN THE WORLD, WHICH MAKES THIS RECIPE RATHER LUXURIOUS BECAUSE IT USES TWO WHOLE TEASPOONS OF IT. THE STICKS ARE GOOD AS SNACKS, OR WITH CHEESE, SOUP, OR DIPS.

1 Infuse the saffron with 2 tbsp of the warm milk and leave for 10 minutes.

2 Sift the flour, salt, sugar, and spices into a bowl, then rub in the butter until the mixture is like bread crumbs. Add the raisins and make a well in the center. Dissolve the yeast in 2 tbsp of the milk and pour it into the well, along with the saffron liquid. Gradually add the remaining milk until you have a soft dough

3 Tip the dough onto a lightly floured work surface and knead for 5 minutes, until it is smooth and elastic. Place it in a lightly oiled bowl, cover with a damp dish towel, and leave to rise in a warm place until it has doubled in size: about 45 minutes.

4 Preheat the oven to 350°F.

5 Punch down the dough, then tip it onto the floured surface and knead for 2-3 minutes. Divide the dough into 12 equal pieces, and after cleaning the surface to make it flour-free, pull each piece out into a 10-inch stick. Place the sticks on a greased baking sheet.

6 Bake the breadsticks for 10-12 minutes. Cool on a wire rack.

variations

To make a single loaf, grease a 1lb loaf pan. After punching down the dough, place it in the pan, cover it, and leave to proof for 30 minutes. Bake for about 40 minutes.

To make rolls, divide the punched-back dough into 12 pieces and roll into balls. Proof for 30 minutes. Glaze with beaten egg and bake it for 25-30 minutes.

2 TSP SAFFRON STRANDS

10FL OZ OR 1¼ CUPS (300ML) MILK AT BODY TEMPERATURE

1 LB OR 3⅓ CUPS (450G) WHITE BREAD FLOUR

¼ TSP FINE SEA SALT

4OZ OR ½ CUP (115G) SUPERFINE SUGAR

¼ TSP MIXED SPICE*

¼ TSP GROUND CINNAMON

6OZ OR ABOUT ¾ CUP (175G) UNSALTED BUTTER, SOFTENED AND DICED

8OZ OR ½ LB (225G) RAISINS

1OZ (25G) FRESH YEAST, CRUMBLED

*MIXED SPICE IS A BLEND OF SPICES UNIQUE TO THE UK, AND EVEN THERE, NO TWO BRANDED BLENDS ARE THE SAME. TO MAKE ONE VERSION FOR THIS BOOK, MIX TOGETHER THE FOLLOWING: 4 TBSP CINNAMON, 1 TSP GINGER, 1 TSP CLOVES, 1 TSP NUTMEG, 1 TSP ALLSPICE.

prune and chocolate bread

I ADORE PRUNES AND WISH THEY WERE TAKEN MORE SERIOUSLY. THEY ARE AN EXCELLENT SOURCE OF VITAMIN A, WITH IRON AND FIBER. THE COMBINATION OF PRUNES AND CHOCOLATE IS HEAVENLY. THIS IS A WONDERFUL BREAKFAST BREAD: IT IS RICH, SWEET, DARK, AND DELICIOUS, AND DOESN'T NEED ANYTHING ELSE WITH IT. TRY MAKING IT WITH HALF DARK CHOCOLATE AND HALF GOOD-QUALITY WHITE CHOCOLATE, TOO.

1LB 10OZ OR 5⅛ CUPS (750G) WHITE BREAD FLOUR
    OR HALF WHITE BREAD AND HALF
    WHOLE-WHEAT FLOUR

2 TSP FINE SEA SALT

¾OZ (20G) FRESH YEAST

16FL OZ OR 2 CUPS (450ML) WATER AT
    BODY TEMPERATURE

12OZ (350G) PITTED PRUNES

12OZ (350G) DARK CHOCOLATE

¾OZ (20G) UNSALTED BUTTER

1 LARGE EGG

1 Mix the flour and salt in a large bowl and make a well in the center. Blend the fresh yeast with 2 tbsp of the water and add it to the well. Gradually add about three-quarters of the rest of the water to the flour and mix well. The dough should be firm and leave the sides of the bowl clean. If it looks dry, add some of the remaining water.

2 Turn the dough out onto a lightly floured work surface and knead well for 10 minutes. You should have a smooth, elastic dough. Return it to a clean bowl, cover with a damp dish towel, and leave to rise in a warm place for 1 hour, until it has doubled in size.

3 Meanwhile preheat the oven to 425°F. Grease two 2lb loaf pans.

4 Chop the prunes, chocolate, and butter. Beat the egg.

5 Punch down the dough, turn it onto a lightly floured work surface, and knead again for 2–3 minutes. Press the prunes, chocolate, butter, and beaten egg onto the top of the dough, then knead or chafe well for 10 minutes, so that they are evenly distributed. You may need a bit more flour if the dough is tacky.

6 Put half the dough in each pan. Cover with the damp dish towel and allow to proof for 10 minutes.

7 Bake the loaves for 35 minutes. They're ready if the base sounds hollow when tapped. Cool on a wire rack. Serve warm.

variation

Make one large loaf and two smaller ones (1lb pans), or free-form two oval loaves and bake on a greased baking sheet. Smaller loaves take 20–25 minutes to bake.

alpine fruit bread

TOWNS IN THE ALTO ADIGE, THE PART OF ITALY THAT LIES IN THE ALPS, HOST OPEN-AIR MARKETS DURING THE CHRISTMAS SEASON, FEATURING A GREAT VARIETY OF ARTS AND CRAFTS. THIS TRADITIONAL CHRISTMAS FRUIT BREAD IS AVAILABLE TO BUY AT THESE MARKETS. IT'S WONDERFUL, PACKED FULL OF GOODIES, AND IF YOU HAVE ANY LEFT OVER YOU CAN USE IT TO MAKE A FANTASTIC BREAD-AND-BUTTER PUDDING (*SEE* PAGE 186).

3½OZ OR A GENEROUS ½ CUP (100G) RAISINS

3½OZ (100G) CANDIED PEEL, DICED

2½FL OZ OR ¼ CUP + 1 TBSP (75ML) GRAPPA (USE WHITE RUM IF UNAVAILABLE)

2½FL OZ OR ¼ CUP + 1 TBSP (75ML) WATER

9OZ OR 1¼ CUP (250G) UNSALTED BUTTER

3 LARGE EGGS

5½OZ OR ABOUT ⅔ CUP (150G) SUPERFINE SUGAR

12OZ OR 2⅔ CUPS (350G) ITALIAN "00" FLOUR, OR USE HALF CAKE AND HALF ALL-PURPOSE FLOUR

¼OZ (10G) FRESH YEAST, CRUMBLED

1 TBSP WATER AT BODY TEMPERATURE

3½OZ OR ⅞ CUP (100G) PINE NUTS

3½OZ OR 1 CUP (100G) GROUND ALMONDS

3½OZ (100G) PITTED DATES, SLICED

3½OZ OR ⅘ CUP (100G) WALNUT PIECES, CHOPPED

⅛ TSP GROUND CINNAMON

⅛ TSP GROUND CLOVES

3 TBSP WHOLE MILK

1 Soak the raisins and peel in the grappa for 1 hour.

2 Meanwhile, heat the water until it is boiling and add the butter. Stir until the butter melts. Keep warm.

3 Beat the eggs with the sugar in a bowl until they are smooth and creamy. Stir in the flour little by little. Dissolve the yeast in the water and add it to the flour mixture. Pour in the melted butter and stir until it is well blended. Drain the raisins and peel and add them to the dough along with the pine nuts, almonds, dates, walnuts, cinnamon, cloves, and milk. Mix well, then put into a large, oiled bowl, cover with a damp dish towel, and leave to rise for 1 hour, until the dough has doubled in size.

4 Preheat the oven to 400°F. Butter and flour a 12 x 16-inch baking sheet, shaking off the excess flour.

5 Shape the dough into four oval loaves about 1 inch high. Place them on the prepared sheet about 3 inches apart, cover, and proof for 20 minutes.

6 Bake for 30 minutes, or until a toothpick inserted in the center comes out clean. Remove from the oven and cool to room temperature on a wire rack. Cut into thin slices and serve.

french spice bread

THIS IS A VERY CHRISTMASSY BREAD, WITH ALL THOSE WARM AND WARMING SPICES. IT IS DELICIOUS BY ITSELF OR TOASTED, OR, AS THE FRENCH WOULD SERVE IT, AS *PAIN PERDU* (DIPPED IN EGG AND MILK AND PAN-FRIED WITH A SPRINKLING OF VANILLA SUGAR AND A DRIZZLE OF HONEY). THE BREAD KEEPS WELL IF IT IS WELL WRAPPED.

1 Put the flour, salt, spices, and sugar into a large bowl and rub in the butter until the mixture resembles bread crumbs. Make a well in the center. Cream the yeast with 1 tbsp of the warm milk and add to the flour, along with the eggs and the remaining milk until you have a dough that comes away from the sides of the bowl.

2 Tip the dough onto a lightly floured surface and knead for 5 minutes, until it is smooth. Place it in a lightly oiled bowl covered with a damp dish towel, and leave it to rise for 45 minutes in a warm place, until it has doubled in size.

3 Punch down the dough and knead it for 2-3 minutes on a lightly floured surface. Press the remaining ingredients onto the top of the dough, then knead or chafe until they are evenly distributed. Shape the dough into two round loaves. Place them on a greased baking sheet, and leave to proof for 20-30 minutes, until they are risen.

4 Preheat the oven to 425°F.

5 Using a sharp knife, slash each loaf three times across the top. Bake for 20 minutes, until they are golden. Cool on a wire rack.

18OZ OR 3⅗ CUPS (500G) WHITE BREAD FLOUR

1 TBSP FINE SEA SALT

1 TSP GROUND CINNAMON

1 TSP GROUND CLOVES

4OZ OR ½ CUP (115G) SUPERFINE SUGAR

3OZ OR 6 TBSP (85G) BUTTER, SOFTENED AND DICED

1OZ (25G) FRESH YEAST, CRUMBLED

10FL OZ OR 1¼ CUPS (300ML) MILK AT BODY TEMPERATURE

3 MEDIUM EGGS, BEATEN

FINELY GRATED ZEST OF 1 UNWAXED LEMON

FINELY GRATED ZEST OF 1 UNWAXED ORANGE

2OZ OR ABOUT ⅖ CUP (55G) BLANCHED ALMONDS, CHOPPED

2OZ (55G) CANDIED LEMON PEEL, CHOPPED

2OZ OR ABOUT ⅓ CUP (55G) RAISINS

walnut and raisin bread

THIS IS ANOTHER CLASSIC COMBINATION OF FLOURS, WITH WALNUT OIL INTENSIFYING THE FLAVOR OF THE NUTS
THEMSELVES. THIS BREAD IS GREAT ON A CHEESE BOARD (SOMETIMES A CRACKER JUST ISN'T ENOUGH AND YOU
NEED A BREAD), AND I LOVE IT TOASTED FOR BREAKFAST. IT LASTS WELL, TOO.

1 Put the flours and salt into a
large bowl and rub in the butter
until the mixture resembles fine
bread crumbs. Make a well in
the center. Cream the yeast with
2 tbsp of the water, then mix it
into the well in the flour with
the walnut oil and enough of
the remaining water to make a
soft dough.

2 Tip the dough onto a lightly
floured surface and knead for
5 minutes, until it is smooth and
elastic. Place it in a lightly oiled
bowl, cover with a damp dish
towel, and leave to rise for 1 hour,
or until it has doubled in size.

3 Punch down the dough, then
turn it out onto a lightly floured
surface and knead for 2-3 minutes.
Press the walnuts and raisins into
the top of the dough, then knead
or chafe in until they are evenly
distributed. Shape the dough into
two torpedoes, then, using a sharp
knife, make three diagonal cuts
through the dough. Place the
loaves on a greased baking
sheet, cover, and leave to proof
for 1 hour, or until they have
doubled in size.

4 Preheat the oven to 425°F.

5 Bake the loaves for 25–30
minutes, until they are golden
brown and their bases sound
hollow when tapped with
your fingertips. Cool them
on a wire rack.

9OZ OR 2 CUPS + 2 TSP (250G)
    WHOLE-WHEAT FLOUR

9OZ OR 1⅘ CUPS (250G) WHITE BREAD FLOUR

1½ TSP FINE SEA SALT

1½OZ OR 3 TBSP (40G) UNSALTED BUTTER,
    SOFTENED AND DICED

1OZ (25G) FRESH YEAST, CRUMBLED

10FL OZ OR 1¼ CUPS (300ML) WATER AT
    BODY TEMPERATURE

4 TBSP WALNUT OIL

5OZ OR ABOUT 1¼ CUPS (140G) CHOPPED
    WALNUT PIECES

4OZ OR ABOUT ⅘ CUP (115G) RAISINS

pine nut bread

THERE ARE MANY VARIATIONS OF THIS CLASSIC BREAKFAST BREAD FROM THE SOUTH OF ITALY: YOU CAN USE ALMONDS INSTEAD OF PINE NUTS, OR ALMONDS *AND* HAZELNUTS. IT'S YUMMY WHATEVER IT CONTAINS. WHEN I TAUGHT IN ITALY, I ALWAYS SERVED IT FOR BREAKFAST; I MADE THE DOUGH LAST THING AT NIGHT AND BAKED IT IN THE MORNING.

3½OZ OR A GENEROUS ½ CUP (100G) SULTANAS (WHITE RAISINS)

JUICE AND FINELY GRATED ZEST OF 3 UNWAXED ORANGES

FINELY GRATED ZEST OF 1 UNWAXED LEMON

14OZ OR 2⅘ CUPS (400G) WHITE BREAD FLOUR

1¼ TSP FINE SEA SALT

5½OZ OR ABOUT ⅔ CUP (150G) UNSALTED BUTTER, DICED

2 LARGE EGGS, BEATEN

½OZ (15G) FRESH YEAST, CRUMBLED

2½ TBSP WATER AT BODY TEMPERATURE

40G (1½OZ) SHELLED HAZELNUTS, TOASTED

75G OR ABOUT ¾ CUP (2¾OZ) PINE NUTS, TOASTED

CONFECTIONER'S SUGAR, FOR DUSTING

1 Put the sultanas, orange and lemon zest, and orange juice in a bowl and leave to soak for 30 minutes.

2 Mix the flour and salt in a bowl. Rub in the diced butter with the tips of your fingers until the mixture looks like coarse bread crumbs. Make a well in the center and add the beaten egg and soaked sultana mixture. Dissolve the yeast in the water and pour it into the well in the flour. Mix the yeast, eggs, and sultanas in the well, then gradually work in the flour to make a very soft, slightly sticky dough. Work in more tepid water if it's dry; you want a tacky dough.

3 Turn the dough out onto a floured work surface and knead for 5 minutes. Return the dough to a clean bowl, cover with a damp dish towel, and leave to rise until it has doubled in size: about 1 hour (or longer if you have time—even overnight in the fridge).

4 Punch down the dough, then turn it out onto a lightly floured work surface and knead for 2–3 minutes. Press the nuts onto the surface of the dough and gently knead or chafe them in. When they are evenly distributed, shape the dough into a ball, then pat it into a round about 8 inches in diameter and 1½ inches thick. Set the dough on a greased baking sheet, cover with a damp dish towel, and leave to proof for about 40 minutes.

5 Preheat the oven to 375°F.

6 Bake the loaf for about 35 minutes, until it is golden brown and sounds hollow when the based is tapped with your fingertips. Transfer it to a wire rack and, when it is cool, dust it with confectioner's sugar.

almond, cherry, and rosemary bread

THIS BREAD IS A MUST WITH A GOOD CHEESE SELECTION, AND IT'S ALSO VERY PLEASANT TOASTED FOR BREAKFAST. DRIED CHERRIES CAN BE FOUND IN SOME GROCERY STORES THESE DAYS, BUT IF YOU CAN'T GET THEM, USE RAISINS INSTEAD. THE RESULTING BREAD WILL STILL BE VERY GOOD.

1 Put the flours and salt into a large bowl. Rub in the butter until the mixture resembles bread crumbs, then make a well in the center. Dissolve the yeast in 2 tbsp of the water and add it to the well. Mix, adding enough of the remaining water to make a smooth dough.

2 On a lightly floured work surface, knead the dough for 5 minutes, until it is smooth and elastic. Place it in a lightly oiled bowl, cover with a damp dish towel, and leave to rise for 1 hour, or until it has doubled in size.

3 Punch down the dough and knead it on a lightly floured surface for 2-3 minutes. Push the almonds, cherries, and rosemary into the top of the dough, then knead or chafe until they are evenly distributed. Shape the dough into a round and place it on a greased baking sheet. Cover with a damp dish towel and leave to proof for 25 minutes.

4 Preheat the oven to 425°F.

5 Bake the loaf for 25-30 minutes, or until it has risen and is golden and the base sounds hollow when tapped with your fingertips. Leave it to cool on a wire rack.

variation
This dough could be made into rolls. Divide it into 12 pieces, shape them into balls, and bake for 10-12 minutes.

8OZ OR 1⅗ CUPS (225G) WHITE BREAD FLOUR

8OZ OR 2 CUPS (225G) WHOLE-WHEAT FLOUR

1 TBSP FINE SEA SALT

55G (2OZ) UNSALTED BUTTER, SOFTENED AND DICED

1OZ (25G) FRESH YEAST, CRUMBLED

10FL OZ OR 1¼ CUPS (300ML) WATER AT BODY TEMPERATURE

4OZ (115G) WHOLE BLANCHED ALMONDS, ROUGHLY CHOPPED

3OZ (85G) DRIED CHERRIES

LEAVES FROM 2 SPRIGS FRESH ROSEMARY, FINELY CHOPPED

pear and almond pain polka

THIS IS A QUICK VERSION OF A BREAD FROM THE LOIRE. IT LOOKS FANTASTIC, TOO. THE BREAD IS USUALLY SAVORY AND IS TRADITIONALLY MADE WITH A *LEVAIN,* A FRENCH STARTER DOUGH. FEEL FREE TO USE OTHER FRUITS AND NUTS, AS DICTATED BY YOUR PANTRY. WALNUTS, APRICOTS, AND FIGS WORK PARTICULARLY WELL.

1 Mix the flour, salt, sugar, and ground almonds in a large bowl and rub in the butter until the mixture is like bread crumbs. Make a well in the center. Dissolve the yeast in a little of the milk and pour it into the well with the remaining milk. Mix to make a sticky dough.

2 Tip the dough out onto a lightly floured surface and knead it for 5 minutes, until it is smooth and elastic. Place the dough in a lightly oiled bowl, cover with a damp dish towel, and leave to rise for 1 hour, or until it has doubled in size.

3 Punch down the dough, then knead it for 2-3 minutes on a lightly floured surface. Press the pears and half of the sliced almonds on top of the bread, then knead or chafe until they are evenly distributed. Flatten the dough into a round shape, then make deep cuts on the top in a crisscross pattern. Scatter with the remaining almonds. Place the dough on a greased baking sheet, cover with the damp dish towel, and leave to proof for 1 hour, or until it has doubled in size.

4 Preheat the oven to 350°F.

5 Bake the loaf for 25-30 minutes, until it has risen and is golden and the base of the bread sounds hollow when tapped with your fingertips. Cool on a wire rack. Using a spoon, drizzle with melted chocolate before serving.

1LB OR 3⅓ CUPS (450G) WHITE BREAD FLOUR

1 TBSP FINE SEA SALT

2OZ OR 4 TBSP (55G) SUPERFINE SUGAR

3OZ OR A SCANT CUP (85G) GROUND ALMONDS

1½OZ OR 3 TBSP (40G) UNSALTED BUTTER, SOFTENED AND DICED

1OZ (25G) FRESH YEAST, CRUMBLED

10FL OZ OR 1¼ CUPS (300ML) WARM MILK

2 RIPE PEARS, PEELED, CORED, AND DICED

4½OZ OR 1⅖ CUPS (125G) SLICED ALMONDS

2½OZ (75G) DARK CHOCOLATE, MELTED (OPTIONAL)

yeast-free breads

THE LEAVENING AGENTS UTILIZED IN THESE RECIPES ARE QUICK, WITH NO TIME-CONSUMING RISING OR PROOFING. HOWEVER, EVEN WHEN TIME IS SHORT, YEAST REMAINS VERY IMPORTANT: BREADS RISEN BY YEAST ARE LIGHTER, WITH MORE INTERESTING TEXTURES AND FLAVORS, TO MY MIND. BUT THE BREADS HERE ARE STILL PACKED FULL OF FLAVOR, AND I HAVE CHOSEN INTERESTING RECIPES. THERE ARE BREADS FROM IRELAND (THE HOME OF SODA BREADS), ENGLAND, SCOTLAND, WALES, ITALY, AND ELSEWHERE.

THESE YEAST-FREE BREADS CAN BE MADE FROM INGREDIENTS THAT YOU PROBABLY ALREADY HAVE IN YOUR PANTRY, AND MOST OF THEM ARE VIRTUALLY INSTANTANEOUS. A SODA BREAD, FOR INSTANCE, COULD BE MIXED JUST BEFORE YOU HAVE YOUR SHOWER IN THE MORNING, THEN BAKED IN TIME FOR BREAKFAST. AND I AM CONFIDENT THAT ONCE YOU HAVE TRIED THE OATCAKES (*SEE* PAGE 163)—THE CLASSIC SCOTTISH FLATBREADS—YOU WILL WANT TO MAKE THEM TIME AND TIME AGAIN. WELCOME TO A WORLD OF QUICK AND EASY TREATS!

fried bread circles

THESE CRISP, YEAST-FREE DISCS CAN BE DRESSED WITH MANY TOPPINGS; I PARTICULARLY LIKE BUFFALO MOZZARELLA OR ANCHOVIES AND OLIVES. THEY ARE VERY QUICK AND EASY TO MAKE AND ARE GREAT FOR PARTIES.

1 Put the flour, salt, and baking soda into a bowl, make a well in the center, and mix in the milk until you have a firm dough.

2 Knead the dough lightly on a floured surface for 5 minutes. Cover the dough in the bowl with a damp dish towel and leave to rest for 45 minutes.

3 Break off small golf-ball-sized pieces of dough and roll them out to very thin disks of about 7 inches in diameter.

4 Heat a large frying pan with the oil and fry the disks one at a time until they are crisp and golden: about 2 minutes each side. Drain them on paper towels.

5 Sprinkle the circles with coarse sea salt and top them with your chosen additions.

8OZ OR 1⅗ CUPS (225G) WHITE BREAD FLOUR

A PINCH OF FINE SEA SALT

A PINCH OF BAKING SODA

4FL OZ OR ½ CUP (125ML) MILK

OLIVE OIL OR PEANUT OIL,
    FOR SHALLOW FRYING

COARSE SEA SALT

bara brith

THIS RECIPE FOR *BARA BRITH,* THE WELSH "SPECKLED BREAD," WAS GIVEN TO MY FRIEND BRIDGET BY HER GOOD FRIENDS RHYS AND JACKY. BECAUSE THE BREAD KEEPS—AND FREEZES— WELL, IT IS SENSIBLE TO MAKE TWO LOAVES AT THE SAME TIME.

6OZ OR ABOUT 1 CUP (175G) DARK BROWN SUGAR

15FL OZ OR 1⅞ CUPS (425ML) MILK

5½OZ OR ABOUT ⅗ CUP (150G) UNSALTED
    BUTTER, SOFTENED AND DICED

1½LB (675G) DRIED MIXED FRUIT

2OZ (55G) GLACÉ (CANDIED) CHERRIES, CHOPPED

2OZ OR 14 HALVES (55G) SHELLED
    WALNUTS, CHOPPED

11OZ OR 2⅔ CUPS (325G) SELF-RISING
    FLOUR, SIFTED

1½ TSP BAKING SODA

3 LARGE EGGS, BEATEN

1 Preheat the oven to 350°F. Line two 2lb loaf pans with parchment paper.

2 Place the sugar, milk, butter, mixed fruit, cherries, and walnuts in a saucepan and simmer for 4 minutes. Allow to cool.

3 When the mixture is cool, stir in the sifted flour and baking soda, then add the beaten eggs. Mix well.

4 Divide the mixture between the two lined pans. Place them side by side on the middle shelf of the oven and bake for about 1 hour. Pierce with a warmed skewer to test whether they are cooked through. If the skewer comes out clean, the cakes are done. Cool in the pan.

marsala fruit-and-nut rolls

THIS IS KNOWN AS *ROCCIATA D'ASSISI* IN ITALY: *ROCCIATA* IS AN ALMOST LITERAL TRANSLATION OF *RUGELACH*, MEANING SMALL JEWISH PASTRIES ENCASING A VARIETY OF FRUITS AND NUTS. IN THIS DELICIOUS VERSION, HOWEVER, THE SLICES ARE LARGER AND THE PASTRY IS MADE FROM A THICKER, MORE ELASTIC DOUGH THAN USUAL.

PASTRY

10½OZ OR 2⅓ CUPS (300G) ITALIAN "00" FLOUR,
   OR HALF CAKE AND HALF ALL-PURPOSE FLOUR

A PINCH OF SEA SALT

1 LARGE EGG, LIGHTLY BEATEN

1 TBSP OLIVE OIL

2-3 TBSP WATER AT BODY TEMPERATURE

FILLING

2 MEDIUM DESSERT APPLES, PEELED, CORED,
   AND THINLY SLICED

8 DRIED PRUNES, PITTED AND CHOPPED

2 DRIED FIGS, STEMS REMOVED AND CHOPPED

2OZ OR ABOUT ½ CUP (55G) PINE NUTS, CHOPPED

8 WALNUTS, SHELLED AND CHOPPED

8 HAZELNUTS, SHELLED AND CHOPPED

1 TSP FINELY GRATED UNWAXED LEMON ZEST

⅛ TSP GROUND CINNAMON

3OZ OR ABOUT 6 TBSP (85G) SUPERFINE SUGAR

5 TBSP MARSALA WINE

FINISH

1 TBSP UNSALTED BUTTER TO GREASE TRAY

ASSORTED NUTS AND FRUIT TO GARNISH

1 To make the pastry, heap the flour and salt on a work surface and make a well in the center. Add the egg, oil, and 1 tbsp of the water and mix with a fork, working in the flour a little at a time and adding more water as needed to form a soft, smooth dough (some flour may remain).

2 Knead the pastry for 10 minutes, then cover with a damp dish towel and leave to rest for 1 hour.

3 Preheat the oven to 350°F. Butter a baking sheet.

4 Put all the filling ingredients into a bowl, and mix until they are well blended.

5 Roll out the pastry into a 16 x 20-inch rectangle about ⅛ inch thick. Distribute the fruit-and-nut mixture evenly over the surface, leaving a 1½-inch border on all sides. Roll up from the short side and press the edges together to seal them. Arrange the roll on the buttered sheet seam-side down.

6 Bake for 30 minutes. Remove from the oven and cool for 15 minutes. Cut into 1-inch-thick slices. Arrange on a plate and garnish with dried fruit and nuts.

rum plum bread

I SOMETIMES CRAVE SOMETHING SWEET AFTER LUNCH OR A SNACK, AND THIS PLUM BREAD USUALLY FITS THE BILL.
IT'S A FRUITY "TEA LOAF" WITH LEMON AND SPICES AND, OF COURSE, RUM—AND IT'S VERY ADDICTIVE!

1 Preheat the oven to 325°F. Butter two 9 x 5 x 2-inch loaf pans and line the bases with parchment paper.

2 Sift the flour, salt, and spices into a large bowl, then mix in the lemon rind. Cut the butter into the flour and rub it in with your fingertips until the mixture resembles bread crumbs. Sift in the sugar and mix in well.

3 Break the eggs into a jug. Add the milk and rum and beat them to mix. Chop the prunes with a knife dipped into flour and mix with the raisins and sultanas.

4 Add the fruit and egg mixtures to the flour mixture and mix well.

5 Divide the mixture between the two pans and spread evenly. Bake for 1½ hours, or until they are firm to the touch. Turn the loaves out of the pans and leave them to cool on a wire rack.

1LB 10OZ OR 5⅓ CUPS (750G) SELF-RISING FLOUR

1 TSP FINE SEA SALT

2 TSP GROUND MIXED SPICE*

FINELY GRATED RIND OF 1 UNWAXED LEMON

8OZ OR 1 CUP (225G) UNSALTED BUTTER, DICED

12OZ OR ABOUT 2⅓ CUPS (350G) DARK
    BROWN SUGAR

4 LARGE EGGS

16FL OZ OR 2 CUPS (450ML) MILK

4 TBSP DARK RUM

1LB (450G) PITTED PRUNES
    (PREFERABLY UNSULFURED)

8OZ OR ABOUT 1½ CUPS (225G) RAISINS

1LB OR ABOUT 2 CUPS (450G) SULTANAS
    (WHITE RAISINS)

*MIXED SPICE IS A BLEND OF SPICES UNIQUE TO
    THE UK, AND EVEN THERE, NO TWO BRANDED
    BLENDS ARE THE SAME. TO MAKE ONE VERSION
    FOR THIS BOOK, MIX TOGETHER THE FOLLOWING:
    4 TBSP CINNAMON, 1 TSP GINGER, 1 TSP
    CLOVES, 1 TSP NUTMEG, 1 TSP ALLSPICE.

quick individual gingerbreads

THIS IS MY FRIEND BRIDGET'S RECIPE AND I AM VERY PLEASED TO ADD IT TO MY REPERTOIRE. I USUALLY MAKE
SOMETHING SPECIAL ON SATURDAYS FOR MY HUSBAND, DAUGHTER, AND FATHER-IN-LAW. ONE WEEK I MADE THESE
AND THEY WERE A GREAT SUCCESS. THAT'S A HIGH RECOMMENDATION!

DRY INGREDIENTS

4OZ OR 1 CUP MINUS 2 TSP (115G)
   ALL-PURPOSE FLOUR

1 TSP GROUND GINGER

½ TBSP GROUND CINNAMON

1 TSP BAKING SODA

4OZ OR ABOUT ¾ CUP (115G) SOFT LIGHT
   BROWN SUGAR

2OZ OR ABOUT ½ CUP (55G) STEM (ROOT) GINGER,
   FINELY CHOPPED

WET INGREDIENTS

4OZ OR ABOUT ½ CUP (115G) UNSALTED
   BUTTER, MELTED

4OZ OR ABOUT ⅓ CUP (115G) MOLASSES

1 LARGE EGG, BEATEN

5FL OZ OR ⅝ CUP (150ML) MILK

1 Preheat the oven to 350°F. Line a 12-hole muffin pan with cupcake liners.

2 Place all the dry ingredients in a large bowl and mix thoroughly. Make a well in the center.

3 Gently heat the butter and molasses together until the butter melts. Stir in the egg and milk. Pour the wet ingredients into the well in the dry ingredients and mix well.

4 Pour the mixture into the individual cupcake cases. Bake for 15–20 minutes, or until they have risen and are golden. Cool on a wire rack.

quick corn and carrot muffins

THESE ARE GREAT TO MAKE WITH CHILDREN BECAUSE THEY REQUIRE VERY LITTLE EFFORT. YOU CAN ALSO VARY THE BASIC RECIPE BY ADDING CHOPPED SALAMI TO MAKE A MORE SUBSTANTIAL MUFFIN TO GO IN LUNCH BOXES.

1 Preheat the oven to 400°F. Grease a 12-hole muffin pan and line it cupcake liners.

2 Sift the flour, cornmeal, salt, and baking powder into a large bowl. Stir in the sugar, Cheddar, carrot, and corn. Make a well in the center and pour in the butter, milk, and eggs. Season with salt and pepper. Mix until the ingredients are well combined.

3 Spoon the mixture into the cupcake liners and bake for 20–30 minutes, until a skewer inserted into the center comes out clean. Cool on a wire rack.

3OZ OR ⅗ CUP (85G) WHITE BREAD FLOUR

5½OZ OR 1 CUP (150G) FINE CORNMEAL

1 TSP FINE SEA SALT

1½ TSP BAKING POWDER

1 TBSP SUPERFINE SUGAR

2OZ OR ½ CUP (55G) STRONG CHEDDAR, FRESHLY GRATED

2OZ OR ½ CUP (55G) GRATED CARROT

1 X 10 OZ (280G) CAN CORN, DRAINED

2OZ OR 4 TBSP (55G) UNSALTED BUTTER, MELTED

9FL OZ OR 1⅛ CUP (250ML) MILK

3 LARGE EGGS, BEATEN

SEA SALT AND FRESHLY GROUND BLACK PEPPER

cheese scones

THIS WAS THE FIRST RECIPE MY FRIEND BRIDGET EVER COOKED, AT THE GRAND AGE OF SEVEN. HER GRANDPARENTS GAVE HER HER FIRST COOKBOOK, WHICH LATER INSPIRED HER TO GO INTO COOKING AS A CAREER. THESE SCONES ARE DELICIOUS EATEN WARM, SPLIT IN HALF, AND SPREAD WITH LOTS OF BUTTER.

8OZ OR 1⅘ CUPS (225G) ALL-PURPOSE FLOUR

A PINCH OF FINE SEA SALT

1 LEVEL TSP BAKING SODA

2 LEVEL TSP CREAM OF TARTAR

2OZ OR 4 TBSP (55G) UNSALTED BUTTER, SOFTENED AND DICED

3OZ OR ¾ CUP (85G) STRONG CHEDDAR, FRESHLY GRATED

A PINCH OF CAYENNE PEPPER

5FL OZ OR ⅝ CUP (150ML) MILK

1 Preheat the oven to 425°F. Lightly grease a baking sheet.

2 Sift the flour, salt, baking soda, and cream of tartar into a large bowl. Rub in the butter until the mixture resembles bread crumbs. Stir in the cheese and cayenne and make a well in the center. Gradually add the milk, stirring with a table knife. Bring the mixture into a ball and turn it out onto a lightly floured surface.

3 Roll out the dough to about a 1-inch thickness and cut it into eight (or more) 2-inch rounds.

4 Place the scones on the prepared baking sheet and brush their tops with a little extra milk. Bake for 8-10 minutes, until they are well risen and golden. Cool them a little on a wire rack before eating them warm.

variation

You can add about ½ tsp of dried mustard powder with the cayenne to make the scones a little spicier. My husband, Richard, loves this!

griddled flatbread

THIS IS A FLATBREAD FROM THE ITALIAN REGION OF EMILIA-ROMAGNA. IT IS OFTEN SOLD ON FOOD STALLS IN THE STREETS, USUALLY WITH A CHOICE OF FILLINGS. I HAVE BEEN WAITING FOR A CHANCE TO PASS ON THIS RECIPE— PARTICULARLY NOW THAT I HAVE A VERSION THAT I REALLY LIKE AND THAT WORKS SO WELL.

1 In a large bowl, stir the flour, salt, and baking powder together. Using a pastry cutter or knife, cut in the butter until the mixture resembles bread crumbs. Make a well in the center and add enough of the water to bring the dough together.

2 On a lightly floured work surface, knead the dough for a few seconds until it is smooth and not sticky. Divide it into eight equal pieces. Roll our each into a 6-inch round about ⅛ inch thick.

3 Heat a heavy frying pan over a medium-high heat and brush it lightly with the olive oil. Cook the dough rounds for about 1 minute on each side, or until they are lightly brown. Brush the frying pan with more oil as needed when cooking each round. Drain the rounds well on paper towels.

4 Sprinkle them with cheese, top with ham, and season with vinegar, oil, and black pepper. Fold in half and eat immediately.

7OZ OR 1⅔ CUPS (200G) WHITE BREAD FLOUR

½ TSP FINE SEA SALT

½ TSP BAKING POWDER

1½OZ OR 3 TBSP (40G) UNSALTED BUTTER, SOFTENED AND DICED

4FL OZ OR ½ CUP (125ML) WATER AT BODY TEMPERATURE

3 TBSP OLIVE OIL

3½OZ OR ABOUT 1 CUP (100G) PARMESAN SHAVINGS

8 THIN SLICES PARMA HAM

2 TSP GOOD-QUALITY BALSAMIC VINEGAR

2 TSP GOOD-QUALITY EXTRA-VIRGIN OLIVE OIL

FRESHLY GROUND BLACK PEPPER

oatcakes

TRADITIONAL OATCAKES ARE COOKED ON A GRIDDLE, BUT THEY CAN BE BAKED IN THE OVEN. THE ROLLING AND CUTTING MUST BE DONE QUICKLY BECAUSE THE PASTE IS NOT EASILY WORKED ONCE IT COOLS. FOR THIS REASON, DON'T TRY TO MAKE LARGE AMOUNTS OF DOUGH; TO MAKE MORE CAKES, JUST REPEAT THE PROCESS UNTIL YOU HAVE ENOUGH.

1 Preheat a griddle on the stove, or preheat the oven to 375°F with a baking sheet inside to heat up.

2 Mix the oatmeal with the salt and baking soda. Pour in the melted fat and mix it in. Gradually add enough of the hot water to create a stiff paste, but be careful—you don't want to use too much.

3 On a lightly floured board, roll out the mixture either into a circle to cut into quarters, or into a rectangle to cut into triangles.

4 Using a spatula, place the oatcakes on the hot griddle or on the hot baking sheet. Bake until they are just browned at the edges: 8–10 minutes. Cool them on a wire rack and store in an airtight container.

4 OZ OR ABOUT ¾ CUP(115G) OATMEAL (USE A MIXTURE OF FINE AND MEDIUM IF YOU CAN GET IT)

A PINCH OF FINE SEA SALT

A PINCH OF BAKING SODA

2 TSP MELTED LARD (OR UNSALTED BUTTER)

ABOUT 2-3 TBSP HOT WATER

irish oatmeal soda bread

THIS RECIPE HAS BEEN MADE FOR YEARS BY MY FRIEND BRIDGET'S MOTHER, WHO HAS PASSED IT ON TO BRIDGET AND HER SISTERS. NOW THEY ALL MAKE IT FOR THEIR FAMILIES. IT'S PARTICULARLY GREAT WITH CHEESE.

10½OZ OR 2½ CUPS + 1 TBSP (300G) WHOLE-WHEAT FLOUR

2OZ OR ABOUT ⅓ CUP (55G) OATMEAL (FINE, IF YOU CAN GET IT)

1OZ OR 2 TBSP (25G) UNSALTED BUTTER, SOFTENED AND DICED

1 TSP BAKING SODA

1 TSP FINE SEA SALT

1 TSP SUPERFINE SUGAR

7FL OZ OR ⅞ CUP (200ML) BUTTERMILK OR NATURAL YOGURT

7FL OZ OR ⅞ CUP (200M) MILK AT BODY TEMPERATURE

1 Preheat the oven to 400°F. Grease a baking sheet.

2 Put the flour and oatmeal in a large bowl and rub in the butter until the texture is like bread crumbs. Stir through the baking soda, salt, and sugar and make a well in the center. Pour in the buttermilk or yogurt and milk and mix quickly to a dough. Free-form the dough into a round or oval and transfer it to the prepared baking sheet. Make a cross on the top using a floured wooden spoon handle, as shown opposite.

3 Bake for 25 minutes, covered lightly with foil. Remove the foil and bake for a further 25 minutes. Cool on the baking sheet.

variation
Grease a deep 7-inch square cake pan with extra butter and lightly dust with extra whole-wheat flour. Ease the dough into the prepared pan and bake it as described above.

note
You can make a close equivalent to buttermilk at home. Mix 1 tbsp lemon juice (or cider vinegar) with 8fl oz or 1 cup (225ml) skimmed milk. Stir and let it stand for about 5 minutes, then use.

whole-wheat soda bread

MY FRIEND BRIDGET'S MOTHER USED TO MAKE THIS REGULARLY BECAUSE SHE HAD EIGHT HUNGRY CHILDREN TO FEED. IT'S ONE OF THE SIMPLEST BREADS GOING AND IS GREAT FOR CHILDREN TO MAKE.

8OZ OR 1⅘ CUPS (225G) ALL-PURPOSE FLOUR

8OZ OR 2 CUPS (225G) WHOLE-WHEAT FLOUR

1 TSP FINE SEA SALT

2 TSP BAKING SODA

2 TSP CREAM OF TARTAR

1½OZ OR 3 TBSP (45G) UNSALTED BUTTER, SOFTENED AND DICED

1 TSP SUPERFINE SUGAR

12-13FL OZ OR 1½-1⅝ CUPS (350-375ML) BUTTERMILK

1 Preheat the oven to 375°F and lightly oil a baking sheet.

2 Sift the flours, salt, baking soda, and cream of tartar into a large bowl. Rub in the butter until the mixture resembles bread crumbs. Stir in the sugar and make a well in the center. Mix in enough of the buttermilk to make a soft dough. Do not overwork the dough or it will become heavy.

3 Shape the dough into a round and place it on the baking sheet. Using the handle of a wooden spoon dipped in flour, make a deep cross in the dough (*see* page 165).

4 Dust the dough lightly with whole-wheat flour and bake it for 30-35 minutes, or until it has risen and the base sounds hollow when tapped with your fingertips. Cool on a wire rack.

note

You can make a close equivalent to buttermilk at home. Mix 1 tbsp lemon juice (or cider vinegar) with 8fl oz or 1 cup (225ml) skimmed milk. Stir and let it stand for about 5 minutes, then use.

red pepper and chili polenta bread

THIS SPICY AND LIGHT IMPROMPTU BREAD IS GREAT TO SERVE WITH SOUP. IT'S COLORFUL, TOO, AND YOU CAN ADAPT THE RECIPE TO INCLUDE OTHER INGREDIENTS: MORE CHILI IF YOU ARE INCLINED TOWARDS HEAT; SOME CHEESE; WHATEVER YOU DESIRE. THE BUTTERMILK OR YOGURT GIVES THE BREAD A LIGHT TEXTURE.

1 Preheat the oven to 375°F. Butter a 10 x 6¼-inch baking pan.

2 Mix the semolina or polenta, flour, and baking soda in a large bowl, seasoning well with salt and pepper. Make a well in the center.

3 Thoroughly mix the remaining ingredients in a jug.

4 Pour the wet ingredients onto the dry ones and stir lightly to combine them. Do not over-stir, because this will cause the bread to be tough.

5 Pour the mixture into the pan and bake for 35–40 minutes, or until the bread is firm and golden. Cool it a little on a wire rack, cut it into squares, and serve warm.

10OZ OR 1⅔ CUP (280G) FINE SEMOLINA OR POLENTA (COARSE CORNMEAL)

3OZ OR ⅔ CUP (85G) ALL-PURPOSE FLOUR

2 TSP BAKING SODA

SEA SALT AND FRESHLY GROUND BLACK PEPPER

1 LARGE EGG

5FL OZ OR ⅝ CUP (150ML) MILK

15FL OZ OR 1⅞ CUP (425ML) BUTTERMILK OR NATURAL YOGURT

2 LARGE RED CHILIES, DESEEDED AND FINELY CHOPPED

1 RED PEPPER, DESEEDED AND FINELY CHOPPED

pies, tarts, and leftovers

THE ITALIANS LOVE BREAD AND SEE IT AS A PRECIOUS FOOD; CONSEQUENTLY, THEY TRY NOT TO WASTE ANY, AND ITALIAN COOKING IS FULL OF FRUGAL RECIPES AND WAYS OF USING UP WHAT IS LEFT OVER. MY GRANDMOTHER, WHO HAD SUCH AN INFLUENCE ON MY COOKING, USED TO SAY THAT IF I WAS CAREFUL, "ONE DAY, YOU'LL BE ABLE TO AFFORD A FERRARI." WELL, I HAVEN'T YET BEEN ABLE TO TREAT MYSELF TO SUCH AN EXPENSIVE CAR, BUT I AM DEFINITELY CAREFUL—WITH MY INGREDIENTS AND WITH MY TIME.

I OFTEN MAKE TWICE AS MUCH DOUGH AS I NEED; I WILL USE HALF TO MAKE MY BREAD, BUT THE OTHER HALF I USE TO MAKE THE CASING FOR A PIE, INSTEAD OF USING PASTRY. THIS IS A VERY ITALIAN THING TO DO, AND IT'S USEFUL FOR PICNICS BECAUSE BREAD DOUGH BAKES TO A MORE SOLID CRUST THAN PASTRY, SO THE PIE IS MORE LIKELY TO REACH ITS DESTINATION IN ONE PIECE. THE TEXTURE IS INTERESTING, TOO, REMAINING CRISPER THAN MANY PASTRIES. THE IDEA WORKS BEST WITH AN EGG-ENRICHED DOUGH, SUCH AS THE PITA BREAD ON PAGE 47.

I ALSO USE UP LEFTOVERS. YOU CAN MAKE A QUICK SNACK LUNCH OR A CASUAL STARTER FROM A COUPLE OF SLICES OF *BRUSCHETTE* WITH A TOPPING; YOU CAN MAKE *CROSTINI* TO SERVE WITH SOUPS; YOU CAN PUT BITS OF DAY-OLD BREAD IN SOUPS OR SALADS; AND YOU CAN EVEN USE LEFTOVER OR SLIGHTLY STALE BREAD IN DESSERTS.

THE MOST USEFUL ROLE OF LEFTOVER BREAD, HOWEVER, IS AS BREAD CRUMBS. THEY CAN BE FRESH OR DRIED (PUT THE BREAD IN THE OVEN ON A LOW HEAT UNTIL IT IS CRISP, THEN CRUSH IT); THE FRESH CAN BE FROZEN AND THE DRIED CAN BE STORED IN AN AIRTIGHT CONTAINER. THERE ARE NO BREAD-CRUMB RECIPES HERE (I DON'T THINK YOU NEED ANY), BUT I USE FRESH BREAD CRUMBS TO BULK OUT MEAT FOR MEATBALLS; TO COAT CUTLETS, FISH, OR VEGETABLES BEFORE FRYING, GRILLING, OR BAKING THEM; OR AS A TOPPING. I SOMETIMES MIX CHOPPED FRESH HERBS WITH BREAD CRUMBS (THIS TASTES WONDERFUL SPRINKLED ON TOP OF A FISH PIE BEFORE IT IS BAKED), AND FRESHLY GRATED PARMESAN WITH BREAD CRUMBS MAKES A FANTASTIC COATING FOR FRESH TUNA OR A TOPPING FOR GRATINS.

olive and anchovy savory pie

THIS PIE IS FROM PUGLIA IN ITALY, WHERE THE FLAVORS OF OLIVES AND ANCHOVIES DOMINATE THE CUISINE.
IT IS EATEN DURING LENT AND THE FILLINGS CAN VARY: I LOVE ASPARAGUS, BASIL, AND PARMESAN.

1 To make the dough, mix the flour and salt in a large bowl. Make a well in the center and add half the oil. Dissolve the yeast in a little of the water and add it to the well. Mix with a wooden spoon, adding the remaining water little by little until a soft dough is formed.

2 Knead the dough on a lightly floured surface for 5 minutes. Divide it into 5 equal portions, cover with a damp dish towel, and leave to rise for 45 minutes.

3 Oil an 8-inch springform cake pan. Roll the first piece of dough into an 8-inch circle. Transfer it to the pan to cover the base.

4 Mix the anchovies, olives, and parsley well. Spread the base of the dough with a quarter of this mixture and drizzle the surface with oil. Roll the second piece of

dough into an 8-inch circle and arrange it in the pan on top of the filling. Spread a third of the remaining anchovy mixture over it. Continue like this, rolling three more 8-inch dough circles, until all the ingredients have been used, ending with a top layer of dough.

5 Brush the top with oil and pierce it with a fork in a few places, then cover and leave to prove for 20 minutes.

6 Preheat the oven to 400°F.

7 Bake for 40 minutes. Remove from the oven and cool on a wire rack. Cut it into tiny wedges (it is very rich and filling) and serve hot or cold.

DOUGH

10½OZ OR 2 CUPS + 1 TBSP (300G) WHITE
   BREAD FLOUR

1 TSP FINE SEA SALT

2 TBSP OLIVE OIL

¼OZ (10G) FRESH YEAST, CRUMBLED

3½FL OZ OR ¼ CUP + 3 TBSP (100ML) WATER AT
   BODY TEMPERATURE

FILLING

26 SALTED ANCHOVIES, RINSED AND DICED

7OZ (200G) OLIVES (ANY TYPE), PITTED

A HANDFUL OF FRESH FLAT-LEAF PARSLEY LEAVES,
   FINELY CHOPPED

3 TBSP OLIVE OIL

cheese, egg, and pepper pie

THIS IS A YEASTED BREAD PIE FROM CALABRIA IN SOUTHERN ITALY. MY VERSION OF IT IS FILLED WITH CHEESE AND PEPPERS, BUT HAM AND BACON ARE OTHER POPULAR FILLINGS. I'VE SUGGESTED CACIOCAVALLO CHEESE, BUT IF YOU CANNOT BUY IT, YOU COULD USE PROVOLONE OR EXTRA RICOTTA INSTEAD.

DOUGH

10½OZ OR 2 CUPS + 1 TBSP WHITE BREAD FLOUR

FINE SEA SALT AND FRESHLY GROUND
   BLACK PEPPER

½OZ (15G) FRESH YEAST, CRUMBLED

6 TBSP WATER AT BODY TEMPERATURE

2 LARGE EGGS

¾OZ OR 1 TBSP + 1 TSP (20G) UNSALTED BUTTER

1 TBSP OLIVE OIL

FILLING

2 RED PEPPERS

115G (4OZ) CACIOCAVALLO CHEESE

2 LARGE EGGS, HARD-BOILED AND SHELLED

7OZ OR ⅘ CUP (200G) RICOTTA CHEESE

1 Preheat the oven to 400°F.

2 Sift half the flour and a pinch of salt into a bowl, and make a well in the center. Cream the fresh yeast with 4 tbsp of the water, then add it to the well in the flour with the remaining water. Mix well to form a smooth dough. Shape it into a ball, cover with a damp dish towel, and leave to rise in a warm place for 1 hour.

3 Meanwhile, for the filling, put the peppers on a baking sheet and roast for 20 minutes, until they are deflated and slightly charred, turning them as they cook. Leave them to cool, then skin them and roughly chop the flesh. Slice the caciocavallo cheese and hard-boiled eggs.

4 When the dough has risen, beat the eggs and melt the butter. Sift the remaining flour onto a work surface and work it into the risen dough with the eggs, butter, and oil. Knead until it is smooth: about 10 minutes.

5 On a lightly floured surface, roll out two-thirds of the dough to fit a 9-inch cake pan, letting the dough come up the sides. Arrange the cheese and egg slices, sprinkled with salt and pepper, the ricotta, and the peppers, in the pan.

6 Roll out the remaining dough to a circle to make a lid and arrange it over the filling. Fold the edges inward, pressing them together to seal them. Cover the pie and leave it to prove in a warm place for 30 minutes.

7 Brush the top with extra olive oil. Bake for 30 minutes, or until the pie is golden. Serve warm.

savory spinach pie

THIS PIE IS USUALLY EATEN ON MAY DAY IN ITALY BECAUSE THE SPINACH REPRESENTS ALL THE FRESH GREENERY THAT IS AROUND AT THAT TIME OF YEAR. IT COULD ALSO HAVE OTHER SOFT-LEAVED GREENS IN IT, SUCH AS HERBS. IT IS A GOOD PIE TO TAKE ON A PICNIC.

1 Put the spinach in a large pot, cover, and cook in its own water over a medium heat for 5 minutes or until it has wilted. Drain, cool, and form it into four balls, squeezing each ball until it is dry. Chop the spinach balls and set them aside.

2 Heat the butter in a frying pan over a low heat. Add the pancetta, garlic, and spring onions and sauté for 8 minutes, stirring constantly. Add the spinach and cook for 5 minutes, stirring all the ingredients until they are well blended. Season and set aside.

3 Butter and flour an 8-inch springform cake pan and place it on a baking sheet. Divide the dough into two portions, one slightly larger than the other. Put the larger portion on a floured surface and roll it into a 10-inch circle that is ⅛ inch thick. Put the circle into the springform pan, patting the dough up and against the sides.

4 Top with the spinach mixture, smoothing the surface with a spatula. Beat the eggs with the cheese and pour over the spinach.

5 Roll out the remaining portion of dough into an 8-inch circle that is ⅛ inch thick. Cover the filling with this small circle, pressing the edges of the dough to seal them shut. Pierce the top with a fork in three or four places. Cover the pie and leave it to prove in a warm place for 30 minutes.

6 Preheat the oven to 350°F.

7 Bake the pie for 30-35 minutes, or until the surface of the dough is golden brown. Cool it slightly, then remove from the pan. Cut into wedges and garnish with cherry-tomato halves.

1 RECIPE PITA-BREAD DOUGH, RISEN (*SEE* PAGE 47)

6 CHERRY TOMATOES ON THE VINE, HALVED

FILLING

3LB 5OZ (1.5KG) FRESH SPINACH, TOUGH STALKS REMOVED, WASHED, AND LEFT WET

2OZ OR 4 TBSP (55G) UNSALTED BUTTER

3OZ (85G) PANCETTA, FINELY CHOPPED

1 GARLIC CLOVE, PEELED AND FINELY CHOPPED

6 SPRING ONIONS, FINELY CHOPPED

SEA SALT AND FRESHLY GROUND BLACK PEPPER

2 LARGE EGGS

5½OZ OR ABOUT 1½ CUPS (150G) FRESHLY GRATED PARMESAN

chard and ricotta tart

THIS TASTY TART IS A LIGURIAN SPECIALTY EATEN AT EASTER. IT USED TO BE MADE WITH MORE THAN THIRTY LAYERS
OF PASTRY, TO CELEBRATE THE YEARS OF CHRIST'S LIFE, BUT MY VERSION IS SOMEWHAT LIGHTER. THE CASING IS NOT
A BREAD DOUGH, BUT IT IS OILY DOUGH, WHICH MAKES FOR AN INTERESTINGLY CRISP TEXTURE.

1 Heap the flour on a work surface and make a well in the center. Add the oil, salt, and most of the water and stir with a fork, incorporating a little flour each time and adding water to create a smooth, elastic dough. Some flour may remain. Divide the dough into 10 balls, each the size of an egg. Cover with a damp dish towel and set aside to rest for 20 minutes.

2 Blanch the chard in boiling salted water for 3-4 minutes, until it wilts. Cool it to room temperature, squeeze dry, and chop finely.

3 Heat 1 tbsp of oil in a frying pan over a medium heat and sauté the onion for 3-4 minutes, until it is translucent. Strain the mushrooms, chop, and add them and the chard to the onion. Sauté for 7 minutes, stirring constantly. Remove from the heat and set aside.

4 Put the ricotta, milk, bread, and a pinch of salt in a bowl, and mix.

5 Preheat the oven to 350°F. Butter and flour a 10-inch springform cake pan.

6 Put the dough on a floured work surface and roll each ball into a 10-inch circle. Place one on the bottom of the pan and brush with some of the remaining oil. Layer with four more circles, brushing each with oil.

7 Spread the fifth layer with the chard mixture. Cover with the sixth layer of dough and spread this with the ricotta mixture. Make six egg-sized depressions in the ricotta and break an egg into each. Sprinkle the Parmesan over them.

8 Layer the remaining dough in the pan, brushing each circle with oil. Pierce the top once or twice with a fork and brush with oil.

9 Bake for 1 hour, or until golden brown. Serve in wedges either cold or at room temperature.

DOUGH

10½OZ OR 2⅓ CUPS (300G) ITALIAN "00" FLOUR,
    OR HALF ALL-PURPOSE AND HALF CAKE FLOUR

4 TBSP OLIVE OIL

2 TSP FINE SEA SALT

2-3 TBSP WATER

FILLING

3LB 5OZ (1.5KG) SWISS CHARD, STEMMED

4 TBSP OLIVE OIL

1 SMALL ONION, PEELED AND DICED

2¾OZ (75G) DRIED PORCINI MUSHROOMS, SOAKED
    IN WATER FOR 20 MINUTES

18OZ OR 2 CUPS (500G) FRESH RICOTTA CHEESE

7FL OZ OR ⅞ CUP (200ML) WHOLE MILK

2 SLICES COUNTRY BREAD, CRUSTS REMOVED

SEA SALT AND FRESHLY GROUND BLACK PEPPER

6 LARGE EGGS

4½OZ OR 1¼ CUPS (125G) FRESHLY
    GRATED PARMESAN

country-style cheese and ham pie

THIS CLASSIC PIE HAILS FROM PUGLIA, ONE OF MY FAVORITE REGIONS OF ITALY, AND THE RECIPE COMES DIRECTLY FROM MY FRIENDS IN LECCE. IT'S A CLASSIC EXAMPLE OF THE REGION'S LOVE OF THIS COMBINATION OF INGREDIENTS.

DOUGH

1 RECIPE PITA-BREAD DOUGH (*SEE* PAGE 47, BUT
   SEE ALSO STEP 1 ON THIS PAGE), RISEN

A HANDFUL OF FRESH FLAT-LEAF PARSLEY
   LEAVES, CHOPPED

2 TSP COARSELY GROUND BLACK PEPPER

FILLING

1-2 TBSP OLIVE OIL

7OZ (200G) PARMA HAM, CUT INTO
   HALF-INCH CUBES

8OZ (225G) BUFFALO MOZZARELLA,
   CUT INTO HALF-INCH CUBES (USE REGULAR
   MOZZARELLA IF UNAVAILABLE)

8OZ OR ABOUT 1 CUP (225G) RICOTTA CHEESE

7OZ (200G) CACIOCAVALLO, YOUNG PECORINO,
   OR PROVOLONE CHEESE

2 LARGE EGGS, LIGHTLY BEATEN

SEA SALT AND FRESHLY GROUND BLACK PEPPER

1 When making the dough as on page 47, beat in the herbs and pepper at the same time as the eggs and melted butter.

2 To make the filling, heat the oil in a frying pan and sauté the ham for 4 minutes. Put it into a bowl to cool. Add the three cheeses, eggs, and some salt and pepper, and mix until well blended. Set aside.

3 Flour a 10-inch springform cake pan. Divide the dough into two portions, one being three-quarters of the dough. Put the large portion on a floured surface and roll it into a 12-inch circle that is half an inch thick. Place it into the pan, patting the dough up and against the sides. Place the filling on top of the dough. Roll out the remaining dough into a 10-inch square with a thickness of half an inch. Cut it into 1-inch-

-wide strips and arrange them as a latticework on top of the filling. Cover the pie and leave it to prove in a warm place for 30 minutes.

4 Preheat the oven to 375°F.

5 Bake the pie for 45 minutes, or until the pastry is golden brown. Remove from the oven, cut into wedges, and serve hot or cold.

bruschette

BRUSCHETTE ARE SLICES OF RUSTIC BREAD, BAKED UNTIL THEY ARE CRISP AND SLIGHTLY CHARRED, AND THEN RUBBED WITH GARLIC AND DRIZZLED WITH OLIVE OIL. THEY ARE A PARTICULAR TREAT IF YOU ARE IN ITALY IN NOVEMBER, WHEN THEY ARE MADE WITH THE NEWLY PRESSED OIL. USUALLY SERVED AS AN APPETIZER, *BRUSCHETTE* ARE ALSO VERY GOOD WITH FISH SOUPS AND PAN-FRIED CHICKEN LIVERS. THEY CAN ALSO BE TOPPED—SEE THE NEXT TWO RECIPES.

6 LARGE SLICES OPEN-TEXTURED ITALIAN BREAD, ABOUT ⅝ INCH THICK

2 GARLIC CLOVES, PEELED AND HALVED

ABOUT 6 TBSP EXTRA-VIRGIN OLIVE OIL

SEA SALT AND FRESHLY GROUND BLACK PEPPER

1 Preheat the grill or a griddle pan and preheat the oven to 425°F.

2 Score the bread slices lightly with the point of a small knife in a crisscross fashion, then grill or griddle them to toast them on both sides.

3 While the bread is still hot, rub one toasted surface of each slice all over with the cut garlic cloves. Put the toast slices on a baking sheet and bake them in the oven for 2 minutes to crisp them through.

4 Drizzle about 1 tbsp of extra-virgin olive oil over each slice. Sprinkle generously with pepper and a little salt, then serve.

variation

Crostini are much smaller and more elegant, rather like the French *croûtes*. In a *trattoria,* for instance, I would be offered a *bruschetta;* in a *ristorante,* a *crostino*. *Crostini* are usually grilled like *bruschette,* but they can be baked in the oven until they are crisp. They are good with salads, soups, as canapés, and for dipping.

caramelized fennel, onion, and olive bruschette

FENNEL IS NATIVE TO ITALY, WHERE IT IS EATEN RAW TO AID DIGESTION. IF ANYONE REMAINS UNCONVINCED BY FENNEL'S CHARMS, THIS IS THE RECIPE TO CONVERT THEM, BECAUSE THE FLAVOR OF THE FENNEL IS MUTED AND SWEETENED BY THE COOKING. THIS VERSION GIVES ONLY ONE EXAMPLE OF A POSSIBLE *BRUSCHETTA* TOPPING, AND THERE'S ANOTHER ON PAGE 180, BUT YOU CAN LET YOUR IMAGINATION RUN WILD AND CREATE MANY TOPPINGS OF YOUR OWN.

1 Melt the butter and olive oil in a non-stick, heavy-bottomed pan. Stir in the sliced onion and fennel and stew slowly for about 45 minutes, stirring from time to time, until the vegetables are golden brown and tender.

2 Add the wine and olives and continue cooking until the wine has bubbled away completely. Adjust the seasoning and keep the mixture warm.

3 Grill the bread until it is golden brown. Spoon the warm fennel mixture over it and serve at once.

variation

Any topping could be used for a *bruschetta:* walnut or arugula pesto, an olive tapenade, taramasalata or hummus, *peperonata* (roasted peppers), *caponata* (see page 88), chicken liver pâté, even sliced tomatoes…

1 TBSP UNSALTED BUTTER

1 TBSP OLIVE OIL

2 ONIONS, PEELED AND FINELY SLICED

2 FENNEL BULBS, TRIMMED, QUARTERED, AND FINELY SLICED

2FL OZ OR ¼ CUP (50ML) WHITE WINE

8 BLACK OLIVES, PITTED AND SLICED

SEA SALT AND FRESHLY GROUND BLACK PEPPER

4 LARGE SLICES OPEN-TEXTURED BREAD, CUT HALF AN INCH THICK

cavolo nero and bean bruschette

BEANS AND *CAVOLO NERO* (BLACK CABBAGE) GO WELL TOGETHER, WHICH MAY SURPRISE YOU, BUT IT IS THE QUALITY OF THE OIL THAT BRINGS THIS DISH TOGETHER AND CREATES THE SIMPLEST POSSIBLE TOPPING FOR *BRUSCHETTE*. DO TRY TO COOK YOUR OWN BEANS, BECAUSE THEY WILL TASTE SO MUCH BETTER.

6 *BRUSCHETTE* (*SEE* PAGE 178)

1LB (450G) *CAVOLO NERO*

SEA SALT AND FRESHLY GROUND BLACK PEPPER

7OZ (200G) COOKED CANNELLINI BEANS

THE BEST-POSSIBLE EXTRA-VIRGIN OLIVE OIL

1 Cut the *cavolo nero* into 2-inch pieces, and cook in a saucepan of boiling salted water for about 10-15 minutes, until tender. Drain well.

2 Meanwhile, heat up the beans in a small saucepan.

3 When the *bruschette* are ready, put them on plates, garlic-side up, and top first with the *cavolo nero*, then with the beans. The finishing touch is the glorious oil, along with a sprinkling of salt and pepper. Eat immediately.

reboiled soup

TUSCANS COOK *LA RIBOLLITA* WITH *CAVOLO NERO*, A BLACK CABBAGE THAT COMES INTO SEASON JUST AS THE NEW OLIVE OIL IS PRESSED IN NOVEMBER. THE OIL IS AN IMPORTANT ELEMENT AND SHOULD NOT BE OVERLOOKED. MAKE AS MUCH OF THIS SOUP AS FITS COMFORTABLY IN YOUR LARGEST CASSEROLE—THE QUANTITIES BELOW ARE SIMPLY A BASIC GUIDE. LIKE MANY OTHER SOUPS, IT IMPROVES IF IT IS LEFT FOR A DAY: HENCE THE NAME.

1 Soak the cannellini beans overnight in cold water. Drain and rinse them.

2 Sweat the onion in a large flameproof casserole in half of the oil. Add the carrot, celery, leeks, *cavolo nero,* and tomatoes and mix so that they are liberally covered in oil. Add half the garlic and all the chili and cook for 10 minutes.

3 Add the soaked beans and stir. Cover with water and then simmer slowly, covered, for 1½–2 hours, or until the beans are soft.

4 Remove a third of the soup mixture and mash or liquidize it to a purée. Return it to the casserole.

5 In a separate pan, warm the remaining oil and sauté the remaining minced garlic with the herbs until it is lightly brown. Add to the casserole and leave for 24 hours.

6 The next day, warm the mixture through, uncovered. It should be wet but not sloppy. Season to taste. Lay a slice of bread on the bottom of a soup bowl, ladle the soup over it, and then pour over a generous amount (don't stint) of extra–virgin olive oil, with a sprinkling of salt and parsley.

6OZ (175G) DRIED CANNELLINI BEANS

1 LARGE ONION, PEELED AND SLICED

4 TBSP OLIVE OIL

4 CARROTS, PEELED AND CHOPPED

4 CELERY STALKS, TRIMMED AND CHOPPED

4 LEEKS, WASHED, TRIMMED AND CHOPPED

9OZ (250G) *CAVOLO NERO,* TRIMMED AND WASHED

8 TOMATOES, SKINNED, QUARTERED, AND SEEDED

2 GARLIC CLOVES, PEELED AND MINCED

1 DRIED CHILI (*PEPERONCINO*), CRUMBLED, SEEDS AND ALL

A HANDFUL OF FRESH HERBS (PARSLEY, BAY, AND ROSEMARY), CHOPPED

SEA SALT AND FRESHLY GROUND BLACK PEPPER

8 SLICES COUNTRY-STYLE BREAD

NEW-SEASON EXTRA-VIRGIN OLIVE OIL

3 TBSP CHOPPED FRESH FLAT-LEAF PARSLEY

tuscan tomato soup

THIS IS A CLASSIC SOUP FROM THE MAREMMA REGION OF SOUTHERN TUSCANY. IT IS USUALLY MADE WITH ONIONS, CELERY, GARLIC, TOMATOES, BREAD, AND BOILING WATER—IT IS CALLED *ACQUACOTTA,* OR "COOKED WATER," IN ITALIAN—BUT THERE ARE MANY VARIATIONS. MOST OF THESE INVOLVE EGGS: YOU CAN POACH THE EGGS IN THE TOMATO BASE BEFORE ADDING THE BOILING WATER, OR YOU CAN BEAT EGGS WITH GRATED PARMESAN AND STIR THEM IN, RATHER LIKE A *STRACCIATELLA.* I HAVE OMITTED EGGS FROM THIS VERSION, BUT YOU CAN ADD THEM IF YOU WANT TO. THE OIL USED AT THE END SHOULD BE THE BEST YOU CAN OBTAIN.

2 TBSP GOOD OLIVE OIL

9OZ (250G) WHITE ONIONS, PEELED AND SLICED

2 CELERY STALKS, FINELY CHOPPED

2 CARROTS, SCRUBBED AND FINELY CHOPPED

2 GARLIC CLOVES, PEELED AND CRUSHED

18OZ (500G) FRESH PLUM TOMATOES

6 MEDIUM SLICES FIRM, COARSE-TEXTURED BREAD

51FL OZ OR 1½ QUARTS (1.5 LITRES)
    BOILING WATER

SEA SALT AND FRESHLY GROUND BLACK PEPPER

3 TBSP CHOPPED FRESH FLAT-LEAF PARSLEY

6 TBSP FRUITY EXTRA-VIRGIN OLIVE OIL

1 Heat the olive oil in a large saucepan and cook the onions over a moderate heat until they are translucent. Add the celery, carrot, and garlic and cook for a few minutes more.

2 Put the tomatoes through a mouli or sieve or grate them directly into the saucepan, stir, and simmer over a low heat for 20–30 minutes to thicken.

3 Meanwhile, toast the slices of bread and put each in the bottom of a serving bowl.

4 Add the boiling water to the tomato mixture, season with salt and pepper, and simmer for 6–10 minutes more.

5 Pour the soup over the bread in bowls and stand for about 5 minutes to allow the bread to absorb the flavors. Serve hot, sprinkled with parsley and with a drizzle of that glorious olive oil.

bread and mozzarella salad

A BREAD SALAD MAY APPEAR SIMPLE, BUT IT'S DELICIOUS. HOWEVER, IT IS VITAL THAT YOU USE THE BEST-POSSIBLE BASIC INGREDIENTS: BREAD, TOMATOES, MOZZARELLA, AND BASIL. THEN YOU CAN ADD EXTRAS TO YOUR HEART'S CONTENT—SOME MORE GARLIC AND OLIVES, FOR INSTANCE, OR SOME GOOD CAPERS.

1 Tear the bread into small chunks. Combine them with the tomatoes, mozzarella, basil, oregano, garlic, olives, and salt and pepper to taste.

2 Drizzle generously with olive oil. Mix well and serve.

1LB (450G) SLIGHTLY DRY, FIRM-TEXTURED, COUNTRY BREAD

2 RIPE TOMATOES, DESEEDED AND DICED

1LB (450G) BUFFALO MOZZARELLA CHEESE, TORN INTO HALF-INCH PIECES

A HANDFUL OF FRESH BASIL LEAVES, TORN

1 TSP DRIED OREGANO

1 GARLIC CLOVE, PEELED AND CRUSHED

A HANDFUL OF BLACK OLIVES, PITTED

SEA SALT AND FRESHLY GROUND BLACK PEPPER

4FL OZ OR ½ CUP (125ML) BOLD, FRUITY EXTRA-VIRGIN OLIVE OIL

fruit bread-and-butter pudding

BREAD-AND-BUTTER PUDDING IS A BRITISH CLASSIC, BUT USING A GERMAN OR AUSTRIAN FRUIT LOAF INSTEAD OF *BRIOCHE* (FRENCH) OR *PANETTONE* (ITALIAN) GIVES IT A NEW SLANT. THIS RECIPE DOESN'T CONTAIN ANY SUGAR BECAUSE THE BREAD IS SWEET ENOUGH ALREADY.

1-2 SMALL ALPINE FRUIT BREADS (*SEE* PAGE 136)

ABOUT 2OZ OR 4 TBSP (55G) UNSALTED
    BUTTER, MELTED

2 LARGE EGGS

5FL OZ OR ⅝ CUP (150ML) WHOLE MILK

3 TBSP HEAVY CREAM

1 TSP VANILLA EXTRACT

1 Cut the bread into half-inch-thick slices and butter generously.

2 Grease a shallow baking dish of about 12 x 8 inches with some extra butter and arrange the slices of bread in it, overlapping them like fish scales.

3 Whisk the remaining ingredients together well, then pour this custard over the bread. Leave it to soak for half an hour.

4 Preheat the oven to 350°F.

5 Bake the pudding for 15-20 minutes. Serve it warm with extra cream if needed.

variation
For added sweetness—if you want or need any—you could spread the buttered slices of bread with some marmalade.

brown-bread ice cream

THE BREAD NEEDN'T NECESSARILY BE BROWN, BECAUSE TOASTING THE CRUMBS OF ANY BREAD BROWNS AND FLAVORS THEM. THE BREADS YOU COULD USE FROM THIS BOOK INCLUDE THE *PAIN DE CAMPAGNE* (*SEE* PAGE 30) OR THE WALNUT BREAD (*SEE* PAGE 46).

1 Preheat the oven to 400°F. Spread the bread crumbs over a baking sheet and put it into the oven for about 5 minutes, stirring the crumbs around occasionally. Watch carefully, because they can quickly catch and burn. Remove from the oven and keep them handy.

2 Meanwhile, heat the sugar and water together to melt the sugar, then simmer to form a syrup, until it begins to brown around the edges. Take the syrup off the heat and stir it into the toasted bread crumbs to coat them well. Put the caramel-coated crumbs on a piece of waxed paper on a baking sheet and leave to set. Then crumble into smaller pieces in your hands.

3 Whip the cream to soft peaks, then fold in the confectioner's sugar, vanilla, and your spirit of choice, followed by the bread crumbs.

4 Pour into a 1-quart freezerproof container and freeze overnight. Rest for half an hour or so in the fridge before serving.

4OZ OR ABOUT 1 CUP (115G) FRESH BREAD CRUMBS

4OZ OR ABOUT ½ CUP (115G) GOLDEN GRANULATED SUGAR

3FL OZ OR ¼ CUP + 2 TBSP (90ML) WATER

18FL OZ OR 2¼ CUPS (500ML) WHIPPING CREAM

2½OZ OR ABOUT ½ CUP (70G) CONFECTIONER'S SUGAR

1 TSP VANILLA EXTRACT

2 TBSP BRANDY, RUM, OR WHISKY

index

acknowledgments

To Bridget Colvin, my great friend, who has contributed recipe-wise and cerebrally throughout the development of this book: Thank you also for the use of your house for the photo-shoot. You are an amazing cook and recipe-developer, and your knowledge and dedication are extraordinary. Thank you. Thank you!

To Susan Fleming, who edited the book: You are always such fun to work with and your outstanding drive and passion to get it right thrill me.

To Simon Wheeler, photographer: You have been the best thing to happen to me over this past year. I'm a huge fan of your work and this book is a shining example. I am very happy. Thank you.

To Jonathan Brunton, photography assistant: A great talent and someone to look out for.

To Geoff Borin, designer: I'm thrilled that you worked on my book—you've done a beautiful job.

To Rebecca Spry, commissioning editor: Clever, hardworking, delightful, and determined.

To Suzanne Arnold, senior editor: Thank you for shaping everything up and for your fine eye, determining the best.

To Richard Moore, my husband and chief taster.

To Rosie Kindersley and Eric Treuille: I love working with Books for Cooks. You are a great source of inspiration, always.

Thank you all.

Ursula

The publisher would like to thank Dany Mitzman for her assistance.